DESTINATION SWITZERLAND: A TRAVEL GUIDE

Georgina Rollins

Table of Contents

Introduction

Overview and Why Visit

Switzerland offers breathtaking natural beauty, from the towering peaks of the Swiss Alps to its serene lakes and lush valleys. The Alps, with their snow-capped mountains and picturesque villages, provide a paradise for hikers, skiers, and nature lovers. Visitors can enjoy panoramic views aboard famous scenic train rides like the Glacier Express, or embark on tranquil boat rides on lakes such as Lake Geneva and Lake Lucerne.

Switzerland is also renowned for its world-class skiing and winter sports. It hosts some of the most prestigious ski resorts, including Zermatt, Verbier, and St. Moritz, where winter sports enthusiasts can find well-maintained slopes, excellent après-ski experiences, and top-notch services. The crisp winter air and magnificent alpine views enhance any outdoor adventure, whether it's skiing, snowboarding, or sledding.

Culturally, Switzerland is a diverse and fascinating country. Its four official languages—German, French, Italian, and Romansh—reflect the blend of influences from its neighboring countries, each adding richness to the regions they inhabit. Each canton offers distinct traditions, local cuisines, and architectural styles, allowing travelers to experience a variety of cultures within one small country. From exploring Swiss art and history in Zurich and Geneva to experiencing the vibrant Italian-inspired culture of Ticino, Switzerland's cultural variety is a major draw for visitors.

Switzerland's rich history and neutrality make it a key player on the global stage. Home to numerous international organizations, including the United Nations in Geneva, it offers visitors a chance to explore diplomatic history and global governance. Beyond the cities, historical landmarks such as medieval castles, ancient churches, and UNESCO World Heritage sites are scattered across the countryside.

For food lovers, Switzerland is synonymous with some of the finest culinary delights. The country's world-famous chocolates and cheeses—especially fondue and raclette—are not to be missed. The vibrant food markets and local restaurants in cities and rural areas alike provide the perfect opportunity to indulge in Swiss gastronomy.

Finally, Switzerland is celebrated for its cleanliness, safety, and efficiency. Its well-maintained infrastructure, reliable public transport, and general attention to quality make traveling through the country seamless and enjoyable. Whether it's wandering through quaint alpine villages, exploring cosmopolitan cities, or embarking on nature adventures, Switzerland offers an ideal blend of beauty, culture, and comfort.

Best Time to Visit

The best time to visit Switzerland depends largely on the type of experience you're seeking, as the country offers something unique during each season. Switzerland's climate varies by altitude, so while the lower regions and cities may experience moderate weather, the mountainous areas can see significant seasonal shifts. This variety means there is never a bad time to visit, but understanding the seasonal differences can help tailor your trip to your preferences.

Spring, from March to May, is an excellent time to visit Switzerland if you're looking for pleasant weather, fewer crowds, and blooming landscapes. As the snow begins to melt, the lower valleys and lakeshores come alive with vibrant greenery and wildflowers. This is a particularly good time for hiking in the lower altitudes or enjoying scenic drives through the countryside. Many popular tourist attractions are quieter during this period, making it an ideal time for travelers seeking a more peaceful experience. Temperatures are generally mild, but if you're visiting mountainous regions, you may still encounter snow at higher elevations.

Summer, from June to August, is arguably the most popular time to visit Switzerland, particularly for outdoor enthusiasts. The weather is warm, especially in the lower altitudes, and the snow on the mountains recedes, opening up the high-altitude trails for hikers, climbers, and nature lovers. The lakes are perfect for swimming, boating, and other water activities, while the countryside is lush and green. Summer is also a great time to take advantage of Switzerland's famous scenic trains, such as the Glacier Express or Bernina Express, as they wind through verdant valleys and past sparkling rivers. However, this is also peak tourist season, so major cities like Zurich, Geneva, and Lucerne, as well as popular mountain destinations like Zermatt and Interlaken, can be crowded and more expensive.

Autumn, from September to November, brings cooler temperatures and a stunning display of fall foliage across the countryside and mountain regions. It's a great time for hiking, as the trails are less crowded, and the vibrant colors of the trees create breathtaking views. The crisp, clear air makes for ideal conditions to enjoy outdoor activities or simply take in the beauty of Switzerland's landscapes. Harvest season is in full swing, so visitors can enjoy seasonal festivals, fresh produce, and local wines in the rural areas. This period also sees a reduction in tourist numbers, which means lower prices on accommodation and fewer crowds at popular attractions.

Winter, from December to February, is the perfect season for those drawn to Switzerland's famous ski resorts and winter sports. The Swiss Alps are transformed into a snow-covered wonderland, attracting skiers and snowboarders from all over the world. Resorts like Zermatt, St. Moritz, and Verbier offer some of the best skiing and snowboarding conditions, with well-groomed slopes and state-of-the-art facilities. For non-skiers, winter is still a magical time to visit Switzerland. You can enjoy activities like sledding, ice skating, or snowshoeing, or simply soak in the festive atmosphere, especially in cities and towns where Christmas markets and winter events bring a special charm to the season. The scenic trains and mountain cable cars operate year-round, so you can still enjoy breathtaking views of snow-capped peaks and alpine villages, even if you're not hitting the slopes.

Chapter 1. Getting to and Around Switzerland

Major Airports

Switzerland's major airports are well-connected hubs that provide convenient access to the country's top cities and regions, making it easy for travelers to explore the diverse landscapes and cultural offerings. The three primary international airports are Zurich Airport, Geneva Airport, and EuroAirport Basel-Mulhouse-Freiburg, each offering a wide range of services, excellent transport connections, and modern facilities.

Zurich Airport (Flughafen Zürich) is the largest and busiest airport in Switzerland. Located about 10 kilometers (6 miles) north of Zurich's city center, it serves as the main gateway for international travelers. Zurich Airport is known for its efficiency and high level of service, often ranking among the top airports globally in terms of passenger satisfaction. It offers extensive flight connections to Europe, North America, Asia, and beyond, making it a central hub for both leisure and business travelers. The airport also has a well-developed public transportation system, with regular trains, trams, and buses providing quick and easy access to Zurich's city center and other regions of Switzerland. Zurich Airport features a wide array of shopping and dining options, as well as lounges, baggage services, and a convenient airport hotel, making it a comfortable stop for travelers in transit.

Geneva Airport (Aéroport de Genève), located just 4 kilometers (2.5 miles) from the center of Geneva, is the second-largest airport in the country. It serves as a crucial hub for international organizations, diplomats, and tourists visiting the French-speaking part of Switzerland. The airport offers numerous connections to European cities, as well as long-haul flights to destinations in North America and the Middle East. Geneva's strategic location near the French border means that the airport also provides access to the French Alps, making it a popular choice for skiers and travelers heading to nearby resorts. Geneva Airport is well-integrated into the Swiss and French rail networks, allowing for seamless onward travel to destinations in Switzerland and neighboring countries. Like Zurich, the airport features modern amenities, including duty-free shopping, restaurants, and airport lounges, ensuring a pleasant experience for visitors.

EuroAirport Basel-Mulhouse-Freiburg is a unique international airport serving three countries: Switzerland, France, and Germany. Located near the city of Basel, this airport is about 6 kilometers (4 miles) from the city center and offers excellent access to Switzerland's northern regions as well as the neighboring French and German cities. EuroAirport's dual designation reflects its cross-border location, with separate entrances for French and Swiss passengers. The airport provides numerous flights to European destinations, with a focus on budget carriers and regional airlines, making it a popular choice for travelers looking for low-cost options. Despite its smaller size compared to Zurich and Geneva, EuroAirport offers all the essential services, including car rentals, public transport connections, and a selection of dining and shopping venues. Its proximity to Basel makes it a convenient option for travelers attending cultural events, business meetings, or visiting the museums and art galleries for which the city is renowned.

In addition to these main airports, Switzerland is home to smaller regional airports, such as Bern Airport and Lugano Airport, which cater to domestic flights and select international destinations. These airports are ideal for travelers seeking more direct access to specific regions of Switzerland, including the scenic Bernese Oberland and the Italian-speaking canton of Ticino. While smaller in scale, these regional airports provide efficient connections and allow for easy exploration of the country's lesser-known areas.

Switzerland's airports are known for their punctuality, excellent transport links, and high levels of cleanliness and efficiency. Whether arriving at Zurich, Geneva, or Basel, travelers can expect a seamless and pleasant experience as they embark on their Swiss adventures.

Train Travel and the Swiss Travel Pass

Train travel in Switzerland is one of the most efficient, scenic, and enjoyable ways to explore the country. Switzerland's rail network is known for its punctuality, cleanliness, and extensive reach, making it easy for travelers to move between cities, towns, and even remote alpine villages. The trains are modern and well-maintained, offering comfortable seating and large windows that provide stunning views of the Swiss countryside. Whether traveling through the urban areas or venturing deep into the Alps, train travel allows you to relax and soak in the landscapes that make Switzerland famous.

The Swiss Travel Pass is a popular option for visitors looking to explore the country by train. This pass offers unlimited travel on the Swiss Travel System network, which includes trains, buses, and boats. With the Swiss Travel Pass, you can hop on and off trains without the need to purchase individual tickets for each journey, giving you the flexibility to plan spontaneous day trips or travel across the country at your own pace. It covers most of the major train routes in Switzerland, including scenic routes like the Glacier Express, Bernina Express, and Golden Pass Line, all of which offer panoramic views of Switzerland's natural beauty.

One of the biggest advantages of the Swiss Travel Pass is that it also includes free or discounted entry to many museums and attractions across the country. This makes it not only a convenient transportation option but also a cost-effective way to experience Switzerland's cultural and historical sites. For example, with the pass, you can visit the Swiss Museum of Transport in Lucerne, take a boat cruise on Lake Geneva, or enjoy discounted tickets to mountain excursions such as the famous cogwheel train ride up Mount Pilatus.

The Swiss Travel Pass is available for durations ranging from three to fifteen days, allowing you to choose a pass that suits the length of your stay. For those under the age of 26, there is a Swiss Travel Pass Youth, which offers the same benefits at a reduced rate. Families traveling with children benefit from the Swiss Family Card, which allows children under 16 to travel for free when accompanied by at least one parent holding a valid Swiss Travel Pass.

Another great feature of train travel in Switzerland is the efficiency and ease of connections. Even in smaller towns, trains run frequently and are well-coordinated with bus and boat services, making it easy to switch between modes of transport. Many of the major railway stations are located in the heart of cities, which means that you can step off the train and immediately find yourself within walking distance of popular attractions, restaurants, and hotels. The seamless integration of the transport system means that exploring even the most remote corners of Switzerland by public transport is hassle-free.

Travelers can also enjoy the variety of scenic train routes that traverse some of the country's most breathtaking landscapes. The Glacier Express, for example, is known as the slowest express train in the world and takes passengers on an unforgettable journey through the Swiss Alps, crossing deep gorges, mountain passes, and picturesque villages. Another notable route is the Bernina Express, which travels from Switzerland to Italy, passing glaciers and palm-lined streets in a single journey. These scenic trains are designed with panoramic windows to offer unobstructed views of the surroundings, making the journey itself a highlight of any trip to Switzerland.

Train travel in Switzerland is not only environmentally friendly but also extremely comfortable, with many trains offering first- and second-class options. First-class carriages provide more spacious seating and quieter environments, while second-class offers great value for money without compromising on comfort. Some trains also feature restaurant cars or snack services, allowing you to enjoy a meal or coffee while admiring the views.

Renting a Car vs. Public Transport

Public transport in Switzerland is world-renowned for its efficiency, reliability, and extensive coverage. The Swiss Travel System is well-organized, with trains, buses, and boats connecting even the most remote areas of the country. The trains, especially, are a highlight of

Swiss transport, offering clean, punctual, and scenic routes across the entire country. Travelers can easily reach major cities like Zurich, Geneva, and Lucerne, as well as alpine villages and mountain resorts. The Swiss Travel Pass makes it even more convenient, allowing unlimited travel on the country's network of trains, buses, and boats, along with free or discounted entry to many attractions. Using public transport also allows you to sit back and enjoy the stunning landscapes, such as mountain passes and lakes, without worrying about navigation or road conditions.

Switzerland's trains are particularly famous for their scenic routes. The Glacier Express, Bernina Express, and GoldenPass Line are just a few examples of breathtaking train journeys that showcase the country's dramatic alpine beauty. Train stations are conveniently located near city centers, making it easy to get around without needing to rent a car. Additionally, public transport is environmentally friendly and allows visitors to travel sustainably, which aligns with Switzerland's commitment to green tourism.

On the other hand, renting a car in Switzerland offers a different type of freedom. While public transport is comprehensive, renting a car allows travelers to explore more remote or less frequented destinations that may not be as easily accessible by train or bus. This includes charming rural villages, hidden lakes, and mountain roads that provide unique viewpoints. A car can also offer more flexibility when it comes to time management, as you won't need to adhere to train or bus schedules. For families or groups, renting a car may also be more cost-effective, especially if you're traveling with a lot of luggage or sporting equipment like skis.

Driving in Switzerland is generally a pleasant experience, as the roads are well-maintained and the signage is clear. However, there are some important considerations for renting a car. First, Switzerland has many mountainous regions, and driving on steep, winding roads can be challenging, especially in winter when snow and ice are common. Winter tires are mandatory in some areas, and carrying snow chains may be required if you plan to drive in alpine regions during the colder months. There are also numerous tolls and vignettes (road taxes) that must be purchased for driving on highways, which may add to the cost of your trip.

Parking in cities can also be expensive and difficult to find, especially in popular tourist areas. Most Swiss cities are designed with pedestrians and public transport in mind, and many central areas restrict car access. For this reason, driving within cities like Zurich or Geneva may not be as convenient as using public transport, and renting a car may be more useful for rural or alpine excursions.

Ultimately, the choice between renting a car and relying on public transport in Switzerland depends on your travel preferences. If you prefer a more laid-back experience where you can enjoy the country's well-connected transport network, admire the scenery from a train window, and travel sustainably, public transport is the ideal option. On the other hand, if you want the flexibility to explore off-the-beaten-path destinations and craft your own schedule, renting a car offers more freedom and versatility, particularly in regions where public transport might not be as frequent or direct.

Driving Tips for Switzerland

Driving in Switzerland is an enjoyable experience, offering some of the most scenic routes in Europe, but it also requires an understanding of local road rules and conditions to ensure a smooth and safe journey. The first thing to know is that Switzerland drives on the right-hand side of the road. This is similar to most European countries, and if you're coming from a country that drives on the left, it might take some time to adjust.

Switzerland has a well-maintained road network, and highways are typically in excellent condition. However, using the highways requires a vignette, which is a toll sticker that must be displayed on your vehicle's windshield. You can purchase the vignette at border crossings, gas stations, or post offices, and it's valid for the entire year. Driving without a vignette can result in a hefty fine.

Speed limits are strictly enforced in Switzerland, and there are speed cameras throughout the country. The general speed limit is 120 km/h (75 mph) on highways, 80 km/h (50 mph) on rural roads, and 50 km/h (31 mph) in urban areas, although you should always pay attention to signs as limits can vary. Fines for speeding are significant, and they can increase sharply if you're caught driving well over the limit. Also, radar detectors are illegal, and even possessing one can lead to fines.

Switzerland is known for its mountainous terrain, so if you plan to drive in the Alps, be prepared for steep and winding roads. These roads can be narrow, with hairpin turns and steep drops, making it essential to drive with caution, particularly in winter when snow and ice can make conditions challenging. In the colder months, winter tires are required by law, and snow chains may be necessary for some mountain roads. Roads are generally well-cleared, but always check the weather forecast and road conditions before setting out.

In Switzerland, it's mandatory to give way to traffic coming from the right at intersections unless otherwise indicated. On mountain roads, vehicles driving uphill have the right of way, as it is harder for them to stop and restart on a steep incline. Be mindful of cyclists, especially in cities and on rural roads, as they are common and have the right to use the road. Also, pedestrians always have the right of way at crosswalks, so be sure to stop if you see someone waiting to cross.

Parking in Swiss cities can be a challenge, especially in busy areas. Most parking areas are either metered or marked by different colored zones. White zones are designated parking spaces where you pay at a meter, blue zones are free for limited periods (usually one hour), and yellow zones are reserved for residents or businesses. Always check signage to avoid parking fines. In rural areas or small towns, parking is generally more accessible, but still, make sure you're not blocking driveways or parking in restricted areas.

Alcohol limits for drivers are strict in Switzerland. The legal blood alcohol limit is 0.05%, which is lower than in many other countries. For new drivers with less than three years of driving experience, the limit is even stricter at 0.01%. Police conduct random breathalyzer tests, and penalties for drunk driving are severe, including high fines, license suspension, or even imprisonment in serious cases. It's best to avoid drinking any alcohol if you plan to drive.

Switzerland's tunnels are famous for their length and engineering. The Gotthard Tunnel, one of the longest road tunnels in the world, spans over 16 kilometers (10 miles) and can be intimidating for first-time drivers. Make sure to maintain a safe distance from other vehicles in tunnels, and never overtake. In case of heavy traffic, expect some delays, as these tunnels can become congested, especially during holiday seasons.

Using a GPS or navigation system is highly recommended when driving in Switzerland, particularly in the mountains, where cell phone reception may be unreliable. While road signs are clear and in multiple languages, a GPS will help you find the quickest routes and avoid getting lost in remote areas.

Chapter 2. Top Cities and Destinations

Zurich: Switzerland's Financial Hub

Zurich, the largest city in Switzerland, is often referred to as the country's financial hub, a designation that reflects its significant role in global finance, banking, and commerce. Nestled at the northern end of Lake Zurich and surrounded by picturesque mountains, this vibrant city offers a unique blend of modernity and tradition, making it a captivating destination for both business and leisure travelers.

The city's prominence as a financial center can be traced back to its strategic location in the heart of Europe, providing easy access to international markets. Zurich is home to some of the world's largest banks and financial institutions, including UBS and Credit Suisse, which have established the city as a key player in global finance. The Zurich Stock Exchange, one of the oldest in the world, serves as a vital platform for trading securities, further solidifying the city's reputation as a financial powerhouse. The presence of numerous fintech companies and startups also highlights Zurich's commitment to innovation and adaptation in the rapidly evolving financial landscape.

Beyond its financial prowess, Zurich boasts a rich cultural heritage that adds to its charm. The city is a melting pot of art, music, and history, with a thriving arts scene that attracts creatives from around the globe. Museums, galleries, and theaters abound, showcasing both classical and contemporary works. The Kunsthaus Zurich, for example, houses an impressive collection of Swiss and international art, while the Swiss National Museum provides insights into the country's history and cultural evolution.

Strolling through Zurich's Old Town (Altstadt), visitors are greeted by narrow, winding streets lined with beautifully preserved medieval buildings, historic churches, and charming squares. The iconic Grossmünster, with its twin towers, is a significant landmark that offers breathtaking views of the city from its tower. Nearby, the Fraumünster church is famous for its stunning stained glass windows created by renowned artist Marc Chagall, adding an artistic dimension to the city's spiritual heritage.

Culinary experiences in Zurich are as diverse as its cultural offerings. The city is home to a range of dining establishments, from Michelin-starred restaurants to cozy cafes and traditional Swiss eateries. Visitors can savor local specialties such as Zürcher Geschnetzeltes, a creamy veal dish served with rösti, and indulge in delectable Swiss chocolates that are renowned worldwide. The city's vibrant food scene is complemented by its numerous markets, where fresh produce, artisanal products, and international delicacies can be found.

Zurich is also a city that values green spaces and outdoor activities. The shores of Lake Zurich are lined with promenades and parks, providing residents and visitors with opportunities for relaxation, picnicking, or enjoying water sports. The nearby Uetliberg mountain offers hiking trails and panoramic views of the city and surrounding Alps, making it a popular destination for those seeking a dose of nature without straying far from the urban environment.

In addition to its financial and cultural offerings, Zurich serves as a major transportation hub, with excellent connectivity to other Swiss cities and European destinations. The Zurich Hauptbahnhof (main train station) is one of the busiest in Europe, providing efficient rail services that make it easy to explore the rest of the country or travel abroad. The city's well-developed public transportation system, including trams and buses, ensures that getting around is convenient and straightforward.

As a cosmopolitan city that balances a strong economic foundation with rich cultural experiences, Zurich embodies the essence of Switzerland itself. Whether you are visiting for business or leisure, Zurich offers an array of attractions and activities that cater to diverse interests, making it a must-visit destination in Switzerland.

Geneva: International Organizations and Culture

Geneva, often referred to as the "Capital of Peace," is a vibrant city located on the shores of Lake Geneva, surrounded by the stunning backdrop of the Alps and Jura mountains. It is renowned for its pivotal role in international diplomacy, being home to numerous international organizations, including the United Nations Office at Geneva, the World Health Organization, and the International Red Cross. The city's status as a hub for global governance has made it a focal point for negotiations, discussions, and decision-making on some of the world's most pressing issues, from human rights to public health.

The United Nations Office in Geneva is one of the four major offices of the UN and serves as a key platform for diplomacy and dialogue among member states. Within its halls, significant treaties and resolutions have been drafted, reflecting Geneva's influence on global policies. Visitors to the city can tour the Palais des Nations, the UN's European headquarters, where they can learn about the history and workings of the organization while standing in rooms where monumental decisions have been made.

Geneva's multicultural atmosphere is palpable, with over 40% of its population composed of expatriates and diplomats. This diversity enriches the local culture, creating a cosmopolitan environment where different languages, traditions, and cuisines converge. The city's neighborhoods reflect this mix, with areas like Carouge showcasing Mediterranean-inspired architecture and a vibrant arts scene, while the old town offers a glimpse into Geneva's rich history through its narrow cobblestone streets and historic buildings, such as St. Pierre Cathedral.

Culturally, Geneva is a treasure trove of art, music, and literature. The city is home to several museums and galleries that celebrate both local and international artists. The Museum of Art and History, for example, houses an extensive collection ranging from ancient artifacts to contemporary art. Additionally, the city hosts numerous festivals throughout the year, such as the Geneva International Music Competition and the Fête de la Musique, which highlight its dedication to the arts and its vibrant cultural scene.

The culinary landscape of Geneva is equally diverse, with a wide array of restaurants offering international cuisine alongside traditional Swiss dishes. Visitors can indulge in fondue and raclette, but they can also explore flavors from around the world, reflecting the city's multicultural influences. The local markets, such as the Plainpalais Market, provide an opportunity to taste fresh produce and regional specialties, while also showcasing Geneva's commitment to sustainability and local agriculture.

Geneva's commitment to peace and humanitarian efforts is further highlighted by its role in hosting various global initiatives aimed at improving lives worldwide. The International Red Cross, founded in Geneva in 1863, plays a critical role in humanitarian relief efforts, and its headquarters, along with the International Red Cross and Red Crescent Museum, draws visitors eager to learn about the organization's mission and impact.

The city's picturesque setting, with the iconic Jet d'Eau fountain, lush parks, and serene lakefront promenades, invites visitors to enjoy outdoor activities and soak in the natural beauty that surrounds Geneva. The lake offers opportunities for sailing, swimming, and leisurely strolls along the water's edge, while the nearby mountains provide numerous hiking trails and winter sports activities.

Geneva stands as a symbol of international cooperation and cultural richness. Its significance as a hub for diplomacy is matched by its vibrant arts scene, diverse culinary offerings, and breathtaking natural landscapes. The blend of international organizations and local culture makes Geneva not just a city of political importance, but a dynamic destination that reflects the complexities of global interaction and the beauty of human expression. Whether one is drawn by its diplomatic stature, cultural vibrancy, or stunning scenery, Geneva promises a unique and enriching experience for every visitor.

Lucerne: History and Scenic Beauty

Lucerne, nestled at the foot of the Swiss Alps, is a city that embodies the charm and scenic beauty that Switzerland is renowned for. Founded in the early 9th century, Lucerne has a rich history that intertwines with the development of Switzerland as a nation. The city began as a small fishing village, gradually evolving into a significant trade hub due to its strategic location along the trade routes between Germany and Italy. Its picturesque setting alongside Lake Lucerne, with the majestic mountains as a backdrop, made it an attractive destination for travelers and traders alike.

One of the defining moments in Lucerne's history came in 1332 when it joined the Swiss Confederation. This alliance provided the city with military protection and economic stability, fostering its growth into a prosperous urban center. The medieval architecture that remains today reflects this era, with well-preserved buildings showcasing Gothic and Renaissance styles. The Chapel Bridge (Kapellbrücke), constructed in the 14th century, is perhaps the most iconic landmark in Lucerne. This wooden bridge, adorned with colorful paintings depicting the city's history, is a testament to Lucerne's medieval heritage and is one of the oldest wooden covered bridges in Europe.

As the city grew, so did its cultural significance. The development of the arts flourished during the Renaissance, leading to the establishment of numerous cultural institutions. Today, Lucerne is home to a variety of museums, theaters, and galleries, making it a cultural hotspot in Switzerland. The Rosengart Collection, featuring works by Picasso and Klee, is one of the notable attractions, drawing art enthusiasts from around the world.

The scenic beauty of Lucerne is undeniably captivating. The city is surrounded by mountains, with the iconic peaks of Pilatus and Rigi offering stunning views and outdoor activities. Visitors can take a cogwheel train up Mount Pilatus or a scenic cable car ride to Mount Rigi, both of which provide breathtaking panoramas of the surrounding landscape. The lakeside promenade is perfect for leisurely strolls, offering picturesque views of the lake and the mountains that frame it. In the warmer months, the area comes alive with flowers, and people can be seen enjoying picnics, boat rides, and water sports.

Lucerne also hosts several festivals and events throughout the year that celebrate its vibrant culture and history. The Lucerne Festival, held annually, attracts classical music lovers with performances from world-renowned orchestras and artists. The city's rich tradition in music and arts is evident in the many performances and exhibitions held in its theaters and concert halls, such as the KKL Luzern, an architectural masterpiece designed by Jean Nouvel.

Lucerne serves as a gateway to some of Switzerland's most stunning natural attractions. From here, visitors can easily access nearby mountain resorts, hiking trails, and ski areas. The surrounding region, known for its picturesque villages and breathtaking landscapes, offers endless opportunities for outdoor adventures, from hiking in summer to skiing in winter.

Interlaken: Adventure Sports Capital

Interlaken, nestled between the stunning lakes of Thun and Brienz and framed by the majestic peaks of the Eiger, Mönch, and Jungfrau, is often referred to as the adventure sports capital of Switzerland. This picturesque town serves as a gateway to the breathtaking Bernese Oberland region and has earned its reputation for being a hub of outdoor activities, drawing thrill-seekers and nature enthusiasts from around the globe.

One of the most significant attractions of Interlaken is its unparalleled range of adventure sports. The region's diverse topography and favorable climate create an ideal playground for a multitude of outdoor pursuits, making it a year-round destination. During the summer months, visitors flock to Interlaken to partake in activities such as paragliding, canyoning, and white-water rafting.

Paragliding offers an exhilarating experience as adventurers soar high above the valleys, enjoying panoramic views of the surrounding mountains and lakes. The sensation of gliding through the crisp alpine air, with the breathtaking landscape unfolding below, is an unforgettable experience.

Canyoning is another popular adventure sport in Interlaken, where participants navigate through steep canyons by jumping, sliding, and abseiling down waterfalls. This adrenaline-pumping activity allows thrill-seekers to immerse themselves in nature while experiencing the region's stunning geological formations. For those who prefer water activities, the local rivers, such as the Lütschine, provide the perfect setting for white-water rafting. Guided tours take participants through thrilling rapids, ensuring a heart-pounding adventure surrounded by spectacular scenery.

In the winter months, Interlaken transforms into a snowy wonderland, attracting skiing and snowboarding enthusiasts to its nearby resorts. The Jungfrau region boasts an extensive network of ski slopes suitable for all skill levels. The convenience of having multiple ski areas accessible from Interlaken allows visitors to explore a variety of terrains, from beginner-friendly slopes to challenging runs for seasoned experts. In addition to traditional skiing, winter sports enthusiasts can engage in activities such as snowshoeing, sledding, and even ice climbing, providing diverse options for adventure amid the stunning alpine landscape.

Interlaken is also home to several reputable adventure sports companies that offer guided experiences, equipment rentals, and training for those looking to try something new. This ensures that even beginners can safely partake in exhilarating activities under the guidance of experienced instructors. The vibrant local community has embraced this adventurous spirit, resulting in a lively atmosphere filled with energy and excitement.

Beyond the adventure sports, Interlaken's stunning natural beauty provides the perfect backdrop for relaxation and exploration. Visitors can take leisurely walks along the shores of Lake Thun or Lake Brienz, enjoying the tranquil ambiance and breathtaking views. The nearby Harder Kulm, accessible by a funicular, offers a spectacular vantage point of the region, showcasing the grandeur of the Alps and the lush green valleys below. This peaceful retreat provides a stark contrast to the adrenaline-filled activities, allowing travelers to unwind and appreciate the serene surroundings.

Interlaken's central location makes it an excellent base for further exploration of the Bernese Oberland. Day trips to the iconic Jungfraujoch, often referred to as the "Top of Europe," are easily accessible from Interlaken. Here, visitors can marvel at the breathtaking glacier views and experience high-altitude adventures such as skiing or snowboarding on the slopes of the Aletsch Glacier.

Bern: A UNESCO World Heritage Capital

Bern, the capital of Switzerland, is a city steeped in history and cultural significance. Designated a UNESCO World Heritage site in 1983, Bern is celebrated for its well-preserved medieval city center, which provides a fascinating glimpse into the country's past. The charm of Bern lies in its blend of historical architecture, vibrant culture, and picturesque landscapes.

The Old Town of Bern is a remarkable example of medieval urban planning, characterized by its cobblestone streets, impressive sandstone buildings, and iconic landmarks. The Zytglogge, an astronomical clock tower dating back to the 13th century, serves as a central point in the city, drawing visitors with its captivating mechanical show at the hour. Nearby, the Bundeshaus, or Federal Palace, is a striking neoclassical building that houses the Swiss Federal Assembly and the Federal Council. This majestic structure not only serves as the seat of government but also stands as a symbol of Switzerland's democratic values.

As you wander through the narrow streets of Bern's Old Town, you will encounter numerous fountains adorned with intricate sculptures that date back to the 16th century. These fountains are not just functional but are also artistic treasures that reflect the city's heritage. The most famous among them is the Zähringerbrunnen, which commemorates Bern's legendary founder, Duke Berchtold of Zähringen.

Bern's rich cultural scene adds to its appeal, with numerous museums, galleries, and theaters. The Bern Historical Museum showcases the country's history and culture, featuring exhibits on everything from prehistoric artifacts to modern art. The Einstein Museum, dedicated to the life and work of the famous physicist Albert Einstein, who lived in Bern during his formative years, offers an engaging exploration of his groundbreaking contributions to science.

In addition to its historical and cultural offerings, Bern is also known for its beautiful parks and gardens. The Rosengarten, with its stunning views of the Old Town, is home to over 200 varieties of roses and provides a serene escape from the bustling city. The city's proximity to the Aare River allows for picturesque walks along the riverbanks, where locals and visitors alike enjoy outdoor activities such as swimming, cycling, and picnicking.

Bern is also a city of vibrant traditions and festivals. The annual Bern Carnival, known as the "Fasnacht," is a lively celebration featuring colorful costumes, music, and parades that transform the city into a festive atmosphere. Throughout the year, Bern hosts various cultural events, including art exhibitions, film festivals, and concerts, showcasing the city's dynamic arts scene.

One of the unique aspects of Bern is its commitment to sustainability and quality of life. The city's infrastructure is designed to promote walking and cycling, with an efficient public transport system that makes it easy to explore both the urban and natural surroundings. This focus on environmental consciousness enhances the overall experience for visitors, allowing them to immerse themselves in the beauty of Bern while enjoying a clean and safe environment.

As a UNESCO World Heritage site, Bern's significance extends beyond its architectural and historical merits; it represents the values of harmony and balance in urban development. The preservation of its medieval character, combined with modern amenities, creates a captivating atmosphere where history and contemporary life coexist seamlessly.

Visiting Bern offers a rich experience that goes beyond sightseeing. It invites travelers to engage with its history, savor its culinary delights, and appreciate its artistic expressions. The combination of stunning architecture, vibrant culture, and picturesque surroundings makes Bern a quintessential destination for anyone looking to explore the heart of Switzerland.

Chapter 3. The Swiss Alps: A Natural Wonder

Jungfrau Region: Skiing and Mountaineering

The Jungfrau Region is one of Switzerland's most iconic destinations, known for its stunning landscapes, charming villages, and exceptional opportunities for skiing and mountaineering. Nestled in the Bernese Oberland, this alpine region is dominated by the majestic peaks of the Eiger, Mönch, and Jungfrau mountains, which together form a breathtaking backdrop that captivates visitors year-round.

During the winter months, the Jungfrau Region transforms into a haven for skiing enthusiasts. With over 200 kilometers of well-groomed slopes, skiers and snowboarders of all skill levels can enjoy a variety of runs that cater to both beginners and advanced practitioners. The ski areas of Grindelwald, Wengen, and Mürren are particularly popular, each offering unique features and breathtaking views. Grindelwald is known for its extensive slopes and family-friendly atmosphere, while Wengen provides a picturesque setting with charming car-free streets, making it ideal for those seeking a peaceful ski experience. Mürren, perched high on a cliff, offers a quaint alpine village feel and stunning panoramic views of the surrounding peaks.

The Jungfrau Region is not just about downhill skiing; it also boasts an array of winter sports and activities. Cross-country skiing trails wind through the stunning landscapes, providing a serene way to experience the area's natural beauty. Snowshoeing and winter hiking trails are abundant, allowing visitors to explore the serene winter wonderland at a more leisurely pace. The region's well-maintained infrastructure, including modern ski lifts and gondolas, ensures easy access to the slopes and stunning viewpoints.

As the snow begins to melt, the Jungfrau Region transitions into a mountaineer's paradise. The spring and summer months unveil a different side of this alpine wonderland, attracting climbers and hikers eager to explore the rugged terrain. The region is home to some of the most challenging and rewarding mountaineering routes in the Alps. The iconic Eiger, with its famous north face, attracts experienced climbers from around the world, who come to tackle its daunting challenges. For those seeking a less technical experience, numerous hiking trails offer breathtaking views and access to picturesque alpine lakes, lush meadows, and cascading waterfalls.

The Aletsch Glacier, a UNESCO World Heritage site and the largest glacier in the Alps, is another highlight of the Jungfrau Region. Adventurous souls can embark on guided glacier hikes, experiencing the unique landscape and learning about the glacier's fascinating geology and ecology. The breathtaking beauty of the glacier, combined with the surrounding peaks, creates an unforgettable experience for hikers and photographers alike.

Visitors to the Jungfrau Region can also take advantage of the rich cultural experiences available in the nearby villages. Traditional Swiss chalets, quaint shops, and local restaurants serving regional delicacies create a warm and inviting atmosphere. After a day of skiing or hiking, travelers can relax in cozy lodges or enjoy a meal featuring local ingredients, including fondue, raclette, and fresh mountain herbs.

The Jungfrau Region is accessible via a well-developed public transportation system, making it easy for travelers to reach this alpine gem. Scenic train rides, such as the Jungfrau Railway, provide breathtaking views as they ascend to the Jungfraujoch, known as the "Top of Europe." This high-altitude destination features an observation deck, offering visitors stunning panoramic views of the surrounding peaks and glaciers.

The Jungfrau Region is a remarkable destination that caters to outdoor enthusiasts year-round. Whether it's skiing down pristine slopes in the winter or conquering challenging peaks in the summer, visitors are treated to an extraordinary combination of natural beauty and exhilarating adventure. The region's charming villages, rich cultural heritage, and breathtaking landscapes create a memorable experience that showcases the best of what Switzerland has to offer.

Zermatt and the Matterhorn: Iconic Mountain View's

Zermatt, a charming mountain resort village nestled in the Swiss Alps, is renowned for its breathtaking views of the Matterhorn, one of the most iconic peaks in the world. Located in the Pennine Alps on the border between Switzerland and Italy, Zermatt is a car-free village, which enhances its picturesque charm and serene atmosphere. Visitors can access the village by train, a scenic journey that sets the stage for the awe-inspiring landscapes awaiting them.

The Matterhorn, with its distinctive pyramidal shape and soaring elevation of 4,478 meters, is not just a symbol of Switzerland; it represents the quintessential image of the Alps. Its striking silhouette, often shrouded in clouds or illuminated by the sun at sunrise and sunset, attracts photographers, hikers, and mountaineers from around the globe. The mountain has captured the imagination of adventurers since the first successful ascent in 1865, and it continues to challenge climbers today, drawing seasoned mountaineers who seek to conquer its formidable slopes.

Zermatt offers a wealth of outdoor activities throughout the year, making it a year-round destination for adventure seekers. In winter, it transforms into a skiing paradise with access to over 360 kilometers of slopes, catering to skiers of all levels. The region boasts a modern lift system that connects Zermatt with the surrounding mountains, including the famous Glacier

Paradise (Klein Matterhorn), which is the highest cable car station in Europe. From this vantage point, visitors can enjoy panoramic views of the Alps, including the Matterhorn and its neighboring peaks.

As summer arrives, Zermatt becomes a hiker's dream, with a myriad of trails winding through breathtaking alpine meadows, lush forests, and rugged mountain terrain. The area offers routes for every ability, from leisurely strolls to challenging hikes that provide closer views of the Matterhorn and its stunning glacial surroundings. The Five Lakes Walk is particularly popular, taking hikers past five picturesque mountain lakes that reflect the Matterhorn, creating perfect photo opportunities.

The village itself is a delightful blend of traditional Swiss architecture and modern amenities. Zermatt's streets are lined with charming wooden chalets, boutique shops, and cozy restaurants that serve up delicious Swiss cuisine. Visitors can indulge in local specialties such as raclette and fondue, paired with fine Swiss wines. The vibrant après-ski scene and cultural events, including music festivals and art exhibitions, further enrich the experience, making Zermatt a lively hub for both relaxation and entertainment.

For those seeking a deeper connection to the region's culture and history, the Matterhorn Museum provides fascinating insights into the mountain's significance and the evolution of Zermatt from a small alpine village to a world-renowned resort. The museum houses artifacts, photographs, and exhibits that narrate the stories of climbers, the impact of tourism, and the enduring allure of the Matterhorn.

In Zermatt, every season offers unique perspectives of the Matterhorn, making it a destination that captures the hearts of its visitors. Whether it's the crisp air of winter, the vibrant blooms of summer, or the golden hues of autumn, the mountain stands majestically, inviting all to marvel at its grandeur. The combination of Zermatt's stunning landscapes, rich culture, and endless outdoor activities makes it a must-visit location for anyone looking to experience the beauty of the Swiss Alps and the legendary Matterhorn.

Swiss National Park: Switzerland's Wilderness

Swiss National Park, established in 1914, is Switzerland's only national park and a true gem of wilderness in the heart of the Alps. Spanning over 68,000 acres in the eastern region of the country, this protected area is located in the Engadine Valley, near the village of Zernez in the canton of Graubünden. The park was created to preserve its unique ecosystem and promote the conservation of its diverse flora and fauna, making it a sanctuary for nature lovers and outdoor enthusiasts.

The landscape of Swiss National Park is characterized by its stunning alpine scenery, featuring dramatic mountain ranges, deep valleys, and crystal-clear lakes. The park is home to over 80 kilometers of well-marked hiking trails that wind through a variety of landscapes, from lush meadows filled with wildflowers in the summer to rugged mountain terrain dotted with ancient glaciers. The elevation ranges from 1,650 meters to 3,200 meters, providing visitors with breathtaking panoramic views at every turn.

One of the park's defining features is its rich biodiversity. Swiss National Park is home to a variety of wildlife, including chamois, ibex, red deer, marmots, and golden eagles. The diverse habitats within the park support over 80 species of mammals, more than 100 species of birds, and countless plant species, some of which are rare or endemic to the region. Birdwatchers and wildlife enthusiasts flock to the park, hoping to catch a glimpse of these animals in their natural habitat. The park operates under strict conservation principles, ensuring that the wildlife thrives while providing visitors with the opportunity to observe and appreciate it responsibly.

The flora of Swiss National Park is equally remarkable, showcasing a wide array of alpine plants, including edelweiss, gentians, and various species of orchids. The park's distinct climate, influenced by its high elevation and geographical location, allows for unique ecosystems to flourish. The changing seasons bring a different charm to the park; summer transforms the landscape into a colorful tapestry of wildflowers, while autumn showcases vibrant foliage, and winter blankets the area in pristine snow.

Visitors to Swiss National Park can engage in various activities, such as hiking, mountain biking, and wildlife observation. The park's well-maintained trails cater to all levels of hikers, from leisurely walks to challenging mountain treks. Educational guided tours are also available, providing insights into the park's ecology, history, and conservation efforts. These tours often delve into the significance of the park within the context of Swiss culture and its role in environmental preservation.

In addition to its natural beauty and recreational opportunities, Swiss National Park is a place of tranquility and reflection. The absence of motorized vehicles within the park enhances its peaceful ambiance, allowing visitors to immerse themselves fully in the sounds of nature—the rustle of leaves, the chirping of birds, and the distant sound of rushing streams. Campgrounds and rustic accommodations in the vicinity enable travelers to experience the wilderness up close, spending nights under a canopy of stars in the heart of the Alps.

Swiss National Park serves not only as a sanctuary for wildlife but also as a vital component of Switzerland's commitment to conservation and sustainable tourism. By prioritizing the protection of its natural resources, the park exemplifies the balance between human activity and environmental stewardship. Whether one is seeking adventure, solitude, or a deeper connection with nature, Swiss National Park offers an unparalleled experience of Switzerland's wilderness, making it a must-visit destination for anyone exploring the country.

Glacier Express: Panoramic Train Journeys

The Glacier Express is renowned as one of the most scenic train journeys in the world, offering travelers an unforgettable experience as it traverses the breathtaking landscapes of the Swiss Alps. Often dubbed the "slowest express train in the world," this panoramic railway journey covers a distance of approximately 290 kilometers (180 miles) between the charming towns of Zermatt and St. Moritz. The train journey takes around eight hours, allowing passengers ample time to soak in the stunning vistas of alpine meadows, snow-capped peaks, and picturesque villages along the route.

As the Glacier Express departs from Zermatt, travelers are treated to stunning views of the iconic Matterhorn, one of Switzerland's most famous mountains. The train glides smoothly along the tracks, climbing through lush valleys and over high mountain passes. The panoramic windows of the train provide an unobstructed view, making it easy to appreciate the surrounding beauty. Each carriage is designed to maximize the experience, with large, spacious windows that extend to the roof, allowing for an immersive view of the striking landscapes outside.

One of the highlights of the Glacier Express journey is the passage through the Oberalp Pass, which sits at an elevation of 2,033 meters (6,670 feet). This high point offers passengers breathtaking views of the surrounding mountains and glacial landscapes, often adorned with stunning lakes and valleys. As the train descends, travelers will encounter the Rhine Gorge, often referred to as the "Grand Canyon of Switzerland." The dramatic cliffs and winding river create a stunning backdrop, showcasing the rugged beauty of the region.

Along the route, passengers can enjoy a range of services and amenities that enhance the travel experience. The train features a dining car where travelers can savor Swiss culinary delights prepared with fresh, local ingredients. The menu often includes regional specialties, such as cheese platters, traditional Swiss fondue, and fine wines, allowing guests to indulge while enjoying the stunning scenery. The dining experience is designed to be leisurely, ensuring that passengers can appreciate both the meal and the majestic views passing by.

The Glacier Express operates year-round, offering different experiences depending on the season. In the summer, passengers can marvel at the vibrant green meadows, wildflowers in full bloom, and clear blue skies, while winter journeys transform the landscape into a serene, snowy wonderland. During the winter months, travelers can witness snow-laden trees and frozen lakes, creating a magical atmosphere that is uniquely enchanting.

As the journey progresses, the train passes through numerous tunnels and over impressive viaducts, including the famous Landwasser Viaduct, a UNESCO World Heritage site. This iconic bridge spans 142 meters (466 feet) and is an architectural marvel, blending seamlessly into the surrounding landscape. The train's slow pace allows for ample opportunities to capture stunning photographs and enjoy the changing scenery.

The Glacier Express is not just a mode of transportation; it is an experience that embodies the spirit of Switzerland. It offers travelers a unique opportunity to connect with the natural beauty and cultural richness of the Swiss Alps. Whether you are an adventure seeker, a nature lover, or someone simply looking to relax and enjoy the views, the Glacier Express provides an unparalleled way to experience the majesty of the Swiss landscape. It is a journey that leaves a lasting impression, reminding travelers of the breathtaking beauty that can be found in this remarkable country.

Chapter 4. Switzerland's Cultural Highlights

Swiss Architecture and Historical Landmarks

Swiss architecture is a captivating blend of various styles that reflect the country's rich history and cultural diversity. From medieval castles to modernist masterpieces, Switzerland showcases a remarkable array of architectural wonders that tell the story of its evolution over the centuries.

One of the most iconic architectural styles found in Switzerland is the medieval Gothic style, exemplified by stunning cathedrals such as the Cathedral of Notre-Dame in Geneva and the Minster of Bern. These structures are characterised by their intricate stonework, tall spires, and stunning stained glass windows. The Bern Minster, for instance, is the tallest cathedral in Switzerland and offers breathtaking views of the city from its tower. This landmark is a testament to the artistic craftsmanship of the Middle Ages, and its architectural beauty draws visitors from around the world.

Switzerland is also known for its impressive array of castles and fortresses, many of which date back to the medieval period. The Chillon Castle on the shores of Lake Geneva is perhaps the most famous, with its picturesque setting and well-preserved structure. This castle, with its sturdy towers and stunning views, provides insight into the feudal history of the region. Another remarkable castle is Habsburg Castle, which was the ancestral seat of the House of Habsburg, showcasing the power and influence of one of Europe's most significant dynasties.

The influence of the Renaissance is also evident in Swiss architecture, particularly in cities like Zürich and Basel. The Grossmünster, a Romanesque-style Protestant church in Zürich, is famous for its twin towers and historical significance. It played a vital role in the Protestant Reformation and remains a central landmark in the city. The Town Hall in Basel, with its vibrant red façade and intricate frescoes, is another fine example of Renaissance architecture, reflecting the wealth and status of the city during that period.

As the country transitioned into the modern era, Swiss architecture began to embrace innovation and functionality. The Villa Müller in Zurich, designed by the renowned architect Adolf Loos, exemplifies the early modernist movement with its emphasis on simplicity and practicality. This villa showcases clean lines, open spaces, and a harmonious relationship with its surroundings, embodying the principles of modernist design.

In more contemporary times, Switzerland has become a hub for innovative architectural practices. The Vitra Campus in Weil am Rhein, just across the border from Basel, features buildings designed by iconic architects such as Frank Gehry and Zaha Hadid. This campus showcases cutting-edge design and creativity, making it a destination for architecture enthusiasts.

Additionally, the Kunsthaus Zurich, an art museum that houses an impressive collection of Swiss art, showcases a modern architectural style that harmonizes with its historical context. The museum's design reflects a commitment to art and culture while incorporating modern elements that enhance the visitor experience.

The blend of old and new in Swiss architecture is also reflected in urban planning. Cities like Geneva and Lausanne feature beautifully preserved old towns, where narrow streets are lined with historical buildings, while modern developments coexist seamlessly. The Olympic Museum in Lausanne is a striking example of modern architecture, designed to reflect the spirit of the Olympic Games while honoring the historical significance of the site.

Switzerland's commitment to sustainability is evident in its architecture as well. Many new buildings incorporate green technologies and environmentally friendly materials, emphasizing the importance of ecological awareness in modern design.

Swiss architecture and historical landmarks offer a fascinating journey through time, reflecting the country's rich cultural heritage and innovative spirit. From the grandeur of medieval castles to the sleek lines of contemporary structures, Switzerland's architectural landscape is a testament to its diverse history and the enduring influence of its cultural identity. Exploring these landmarks provides insight into the nation's past, present, and future, making Switzerland a captivating destination for architecture lovers and history enthusiasts alike.

Traditional Swiss Festivals and Events

Traditional Swiss festivals and events reflect the country's rich cultural heritage and regional diversity, bringing together communities in vibrant celebrations that honor history, customs, and the changing seasons. These festivals often showcase the unique traditions of different cantons, featuring music, dance, food, and crafts, making them a colorful and engaging experience for both locals and visitors.

One of the most famous traditional festivals in Switzerland is Fasnacht, celebrated primarily in Basel and other cities during the days leading up to Lent. This lively carnival features elaborate parades filled with intricately designed floats, colorful costumes, and masked participants. The event kicks off with the "Morgestraich" at dawn, where the streets are illuminated only by lanterns, creating a magical atmosphere. Musicians play traditional tunes on drums and piccolos, and the air is filled with the scent of local delicacies, making it a feast for the senses. The spirit of

Fasnacht is one of joy and creativity, as locals and visitors alike immerse themselves in the festivities.

In late summer, the Alpabzug or transhumance celebrates the return of cattle from high alpine pastures to the valleys. This tradition is particularly prevalent in the mountainous regions, where herders lead their decorated cows down the slopes adorned with flowers and large bells. The event is marked by vibrant parades, with farmers dressed in traditional Swiss attire, showcasing their herds while sharing local cheese and other delicacies with spectators. This event not only emphasizes the deep connection between the Swiss people and their land but also highlights the importance of agriculture and livestock in Swiss culture.

The Fête de l'Escalade is another notable festival, celebrated in Geneva to commemorate the city's victory over the Duke of Savoy in 1602. This historical event is marked by a lively parade featuring costumed participants, musicians, and actors reenacting the siege. Festivities include the consumption of chocolate cauldrons, symbolizing the defeat of the enemy, and various activities for children. The Fête de l'Escalade emphasizes community spirit, history, and the pride of the Genevan people in their independence.

In the fall, the Swiss National Day, celebrated on August 1st, marks the founding of the Swiss Confederation in 1291. This day is observed with fireworks, bonfires, and speeches across the country. Communities come together to celebrate with traditional music, dance, and food, showcasing regional specialties. The event serves as a reminder of Swiss unity and independence, with locals proudly displaying their national flags and participating in various activities that foster a sense of belonging and pride in their heritage.

The Zug Fireworks Festival is an enchanting event held in the town of Zug during the summer months. This festival showcases spectacular fireworks displays that light up the night sky over Lake Zug. Accompanied by live music and festivities on the lakeshore, it attracts locals and tourists alike, creating a festive atmosphere. Families and friends gather to enjoy picnics while waiting for the fireworks, making it a cherished summer tradition.

Another significant cultural event is the International Balloon Festival in Château-d'Oex, held every January. This colorful festival attracts hot air balloon enthusiasts from around the world, who showcase their stunningly designed balloons against the picturesque backdrop of the Swiss Alps. The event includes various activities, including balloon rides, night glows where balloons are lit up in unison, and workshops for those interested in the art of ballooning. The festival highlights Switzerland's commitment to outdoor activities and adventure tourism, providing a magical experience for attendees.

Throughout the year, many regions also host Christmas markets, where visitors can experience the charm of Swiss holiday traditions. These markets feature beautifully decorated stalls selling handcrafted goods, local delicacies, mulled wine, and traditional treats such as Zimtsterne (cinnamon stars) and Lebkuchen (gingerbread). The festive atmosphere, complete with twinkling lights and carolers, creates a warm and inviting experience that brings communities together in celebration of the holiday season.

Traditional Swiss festivals and events provide an enriching experience for anyone interested in exploring the diverse cultural landscape of the country. They highlight the importance of community, history, and the changing seasons while showcasing the unique customs and traditions that define Swiss culture. By participating in these celebrations, visitors can gain a deeper understanding of the Swiss way of life and the values that have shaped this beautiful nation.

Museums and Galleries to Visit

Switzerland boasts a vibrant array of museums and galleries that reflect its rich cultural heritage, artistic innovation, and commitment to preserving history. From world-renowned art institutions to engaging science and history museums, the country offers something for every kind of visitor.

In Zurich, the Kunsthaus Zurich stands out as one of Switzerland's premier art museums. Founded in the early 20th century, it houses an impressive collection that spans several centuries, featuring works from renowned artists such as Alberto Giacometti, Marc Chagall, and Vincent van Gogh. The museum frequently hosts temporary exhibitions that showcase contemporary art, further solidifying its reputation as a hub for artistic dialogue and innovation.

Not far from Zurich, the Swiss National Museum in the heart of the city presents a comprehensive overview of Swiss cultural history. Housed in a stunning fairytale-like castle, the museum features exhibits ranging from prehistoric artifacts to contemporary Swiss design. Visitors can explore the rich tapestry of Swiss heritage through interactive displays, historical artifacts, and themed exhibitions that highlight the country's diverse regional cultures.

In Geneva, the Museum of Art and History Is a must-visit destination, showcasing a vast collection that includes fine arts, applied arts, and archaeology. The museum's exhibits span various periods, with notable pieces from the Renaissance to the modern era. The building itself is an architectural gem, blending classical and contemporary elements. The **Musée d'Art et d'Histoire** also hosts temporary exhibitions that often feature international artists, making it a dynamic space for cultural exchange.

The Patek Philippe Museum, also located in Geneva, offers a unique glimpse into the world of horology, showcasing the history and artistry of watchmaking. The museum houses an impressive collection of timepieces, including antique watches and the luxury brand's exquisite creations. Visitors can learn about the evolution of watchmaking techniques and appreciate the intricate craftsmanship that defines Swiss timepieces.

In Basel, the Fondation Beyeler is a renowned art museum that features a stunning collection of modern classics, including works by Picasso, Monet, and van Gogh. Set in a beautiful park designed by renowned architect Renzo Piano, the museum provides a serene environment for visitors to appreciate the interplay between art and nature. The foundation also hosts rotating exhibitions, allowing for a continuous exploration of modern and contemporary art.

The Vitra Design Museum, located just across the border in Germany, is an essential stop for design enthusiasts. It focuses on industrial design and architecture, showcasing groundbreaking work by influential designers and architects. The museum's unique building, designed by Frank Gehry, itself is a masterpiece of modern architecture, making it a destination for those interested in both design and architectural innovation.

In Lausanne, the Olympic Museum celebrates the history of the Olympic Games and their impact on sports and culture. Interactive exhibits, multimedia presentations, and historical artifacts provide insight into the Olympic spirit and the evolution of the Games. The museum is beautifully situated on the shores of Lake Geneva, offering visitors picturesque views alongside their exploration of sports history.

Switzerland's commitment to contemporary art is exemplified in Kunstmuseum Basel, the oldest public art collection in Switzerland. It houses an extensive range of artworks from the Middle Ages to contemporary pieces, including an impressive selection of modern art from the 20th century. The museum often collaborates with international artists and hosts temporary exhibitions that explore current artistic practices.

In Bern, the Bern Historical Museum offers a deep dive into the cultural history of the Swiss capital. Its extensive collection encompasses everything from prehistoric artifacts to works by Swiss artists like Paul Klee. The museum also features a dedicated Einstein Museum, celebrating the life and contributions of the famous physicist, who lived in Bern during the early years of his career.

The Musée de l'Élysée in Lausanne is dedicated to photography and visual communication. It features rotating exhibitions that highlight the works of both established and emerging photographers, emphasizing the importance of photography in contemporary art. The museum is renowned for its educational programs and workshops, making it a vibrant space for creative exploration.

Finally, the Zürcher Kunstgesellschaft in Zurich is an essential venue for contemporary art lovers. It organizes exhibitions that showcase cutting-edge artistic practices and emerging talents, fostering an environment of innovation and experimentation. The gallery's focus on contemporary art contributes to Zurich's reputation as a dynamic cultural hub.

Switzerland's museums and galleries offer an enriching experience for visitors, reflecting the country's cultural diversity, artistic innovation, and historical significance. From classical art collections to contemporary exhibitions, the Swiss museum landscape invites exploration and appreciation, ensuring that every visitor finds something captivating and thought-provoking. Whether one is a history buff, an art aficionado, or simply curious, Switzerland's cultural institutions promise a memorable journey through the nation's heritage and creativity.

Chapter 5. Outdoor Activities

Best Ski Resorts and Winter Sports

Switzerland is renowned for its exceptional skiing and winter sports, drawing enthusiasts from around the globe to its pristine slopes and picturesque mountain scenery. The country boasts a myriad of ski resorts, each offering unique experiences, stunning views, and a variety of winter activities that cater to all levels of skiers and snowboarders.

One of the most iconic ski resorts in Switzerland is Zermatt, nestled at the foot of the majestic Matterhorn. Zermatt is celebrated not only for its excellent skiing conditions but also for its charming car-free village atmosphere. With over 360 kilometers of ski slopes, Zermatt caters to all skill levels, offering everything from gentle runs for beginners to challenging off-piste terrain for experienced skiers. The breathtaking views of the Matterhorn create an unforgettable backdrop for winter sports enthusiasts. Additionally, Zermatt offers a vibrant après-ski scene with cozy mountain huts, upscale restaurants, and lively bars, making it a perfect destination for those looking to unwind after a day on the slopes.

Another standout destination is St. Moritz, which is known as the birthplace of winter tourism and has hosted the Winter Olympics twice. This luxurious resort offers a combination of top-notch skiing and high-end amenities. With more than 350 kilometers of slopes, St. Moritz provides a diverse range of skiing options. The resort is also famous for its unique attractions, such as the Cresta Run, an adrenaline-pumping natural ice toboggan track that attracts daring visitors. St. Moritz is synonymous with sophistication, boasting elegant shops, gourmet dining, and exclusive events, including the renowned Snow Polo World Cup.

Interlaken, situated between Lake Thun and Lake Brienz, serves as a gateway to the Jungfrau region and offers access to several ski areas, including Grindelwald and Wengen. The surrounding mountains provide an impressive backdrop for winter sports, with the towering Eiger, Mönch, and Jungfrau peaks looming above. The interconnected ski areas in the Jungfrau region offer more than 200 kilometers of ski runs, suitable for all levels. Interlaken is also known for its outdoor adventure activities beyond skiing, such as snowshoeing, ice climbing, and paragliding, making it an exciting destination for thrill-seekers.

The Engadin Valley, home to resorts like Sils and Pontresina, is another excellent choice for skiing and winter sports. This less crowded area is ideal for those seeking a tranquil experience surrounded by breathtaking landscapes. The region boasts over 300 kilometers of slopes, as well as numerous cross-country skiing trails, making it a haven for both alpine skiers and Nordic enthusiasts. The picturesque villages and the stunning Lake Sils further enhance the charm of this area, providing a serene atmosphere for relaxation after a day on the slopes.

Laax is recognized as one of Europe's premier snowboarding destinations, featuring an impressive range of terrain parks and halfpipes. With over 220 kilometers of ski runs and a vibrant snowboarding culture, Laax attracts enthusiasts from around the world. The resort hosts numerous competitions and events, fostering a lively and youthful atmosphere. Beyond snowboarding and skiing, Laax offers various winter activities, including snowshoeing and winter hiking, allowing visitors to explore the stunning alpine scenery at their own pace.

For families and beginners, the ski resorts of Verbier and Engelberg provide excellent options. Verbier is known for its extensive ski area and lively après-ski scene, making it a great choice for families looking for a fun and social atmosphere. The resort features a range of slopes suitable for beginners and more advanced skiers, ensuring that everyone in the family can enjoy their time on the mountain. Engelberg, on the other hand, offers a more laid-back vibe, with a focus on family-friendly skiing. Its ski school programs are highly regarded, making it an ideal destination for those new to the sport.

In addition to skiing and snowboarding, Switzerland offers a wide array of winter sports activities, ensuring that there's something for everyone. Snowshoeing has gained popularity in recent years, allowing visitors to explore the snow-covered landscapes at a more leisurely pace. Many resorts offer marked trails for snowshoeing, and guided tours are available for those looking to learn more about the surrounding nature.

Cross-country skiing is another popular activity, with numerous trails available throughout the country. The stunning scenery of the Swiss Alps provides a breathtaking backdrop for this peaceful sport, and many resorts offer well-groomed tracks that cater to various skill levels. For those seeking a unique experience, ice climbing and winter hiking provide exhilarating ways to explore the icy landscapes, with guided excursions available in many areas.

Switzerland is a winter sports paradise, offering a diverse range of ski resorts and winter activities that cater to everyone from beginners to seasoned professionals. The combination of stunning landscapes, top-notch facilities, and a rich culture of winter sports makes Switzerland an ideal destination for those looking to experience the thrill of skiing, snowboarding, and a myriad of other winter adventures. Whether it's the luxury of St. Moritz, the charm of Zermatt, or the family-friendly atmosphere of Verbier, each resort provides a unique experience, ensuring that visitors leave with unforgettable memories of their Swiss winter getaway.

Hiking Trails and Scenic Walks

The Swiss National Park, located in the Engadine Valley, is one of the most stunning natural areas in the country. It boasts a vast array of trails that traverse diverse ecosystems, including alpine meadows, dense forests, and rugged mountain terrain. As visitors hike through the park, they can enjoy encounters with wildlife such as ibex, chamois, and marmots, as well as breathtaking views of the surrounding peaks. The trails range from easy paths suitable for families to more demanding routes that require a higher level of fitness, making it an ideal destination for all outdoor enthusiasts.

The Jungfrau Region is another hiker's paradise, featuring iconic trails that lead to awe-inspiring vistas. The trail from Grindelwald to First is particularly popular, offering stunning views of the Eiger, Mönch, and Jungfrau mountains. Along the way, hikers can stop at picturesque spots like the First Cliff Walk, a suspension bridge that juts out over the mountainside, providing thrilling views of the valley below. For those looking for a more challenging hike, the Eiger Trail offers a closer view of the formidable Eiger North Face, along with breathtaking panoramas of the surrounding landscape.

In the Zermatt region, the hike to Gornergrat presents another unforgettable experience. This trail takes hikers to one of the highest viewing platforms in the area, where they can gaze at the majestic Matterhorn and the vast expanse of the surrounding glaciers. The journey can be made on foot or by taking the cogwheel train to the summit, allowing for flexibility in how one wants to experience this iconic landscape. The walk itself is filled with breathtaking alpine scenery, wildflowers in the summer, and the crisp mountain air, making it a memorable adventure for all who take on the challenge.

For a more leisurely experience, the Lakeside Walks around Switzerland's pristine lakes are particularly enchanting. The Lake Geneva region, for instance, offers beautiful promenades in cities like Montreux and Lausanne, where visitors can enjoy gentle walks along the water's edge, surrounded by stunning views of the Alps. The Lavaux Vineyards, a UNESCO World Heritage site, features scenic walking trails that wind through terraced vineyards, allowing hikers to savor the local wine culture while enjoying breathtaking views of the lake.

The Aletsch Glacier, the largest glacier in the Alps, is another remarkable hiking destination. The Aletsch Panorama Trail takes hikers along the glacier's edge, providing stunning views of the ice formations and the surrounding mountains. The contrast of the blue ice against the green alpine meadows creates a breathtaking spectacle, making this hike a must for those seeking to experience the grandeur of Switzerland's natural beauty.

The Via Alpina, a long-distance hiking trail that spans across Switzerland and connects the country's various alpine regions, offers an extensive network of routes for adventurous hikers. This trail showcases the diversity of Switzerland's landscapes, from rugged mountains to lush valleys and charming villages. Walking along the Via Alpina allows hikers to immerse themselves in the cultural richness of the region, passing through picturesque towns where they can sample local cuisine and experience the warmth of Swiss hospitality.

Another enchanting hiking experience can be found in the Emmental region, famous for its rolling hills and traditional Swiss farms. The Emmental Trail takes hikers through idyllic countryside, offering picturesque views of the landscape dotted with charming chalets and grazing cows. This area is also known for its production of the iconic Emmental cheese, providing an opportunity for hikers to taste this delightful Swiss delicacy while enjoying the beautiful scenery.

The Ticino region in southern Switzerland presents a different landscape with its Mediterranean flair, featuring palm trees, azure lakes, and rugged mountains. The Sentiero del Gotthard is a stunning trail that offers breathtaking views of Lake Lugano and the surrounding mountains. The combination of lush vegetation, tranquil waters, and the dramatic backdrop of the Alps creates a unique hiking experience that captures the essence of the region.

Safety and accessibility are important considerations for hikers in Switzerland. The extensive network of trails is well-marked, and maps and guides are readily available to ensure that hikers can navigate their routes with ease. Additionally, many popular trails offer various facilities, such as rest areas and mountain huts, where hikers can take a break, enjoy a meal, or simply soak in the views.

Switzerland's hiking trails and scenic walks provide a unique way to explore the country's diverse landscapes and natural wonders. Whether one seeks the challenge of a high-altitude trek, the tranquility of a lakeside stroll, or the charm of a rural path, the opportunities for adventure and discovery are limitless. With its stunning vistas, rich biodiversity, and welcoming hospitality, Switzerland is a hiker's dream destination that leaves a lasting impression on all who venture into its breathtaking outdoors.

Paragliding, Bungee Jumping, and Other Adventures

Paragliding in Switzerland is a surreal experience that allows you to soar like a bird over some of the most magnificent scenery in the world. Popular locations for paragliding include Interlaken, Lauterbrunnen, and the slopes of the Eiger, where the combination of thermal winds and stunning vistas create ideal conditions for flying. Launching from a high point, paragliders can glide gracefully over the landscape, taking in panoramic views of the snow-capped peaks of the Alps, verdant meadows, and glimmering lakes below. Many local operators offer tandem paragliding experiences for those new to the sport, pairing participants with experienced pilots who guide them through the entire process, ensuring both safety and enjoyment. The sensation of floating through the air while taking in the breathtaking surroundings is a memory that stays with adventurers long after they have landed.

Bungee jumping is another exhilarating activity that draws thrill-seekers to Switzerland. The country boasts some of the highest and most breathtaking jumps in the world, with locations like the Verzasca Dam, which features a 220-meter plunge. This dam became famous after being featured in the James Bond film "GoldenEye." The experience begins with a heart-pounding ascent, where jumpers are harnessed and led to the edge of the platform. The moment of freefall offers a rush of adrenaline that few experiences can match, as jumpers plummet towards the stunning valley below before the bungee cord pulls them back up, creating an exhilarating rebound effect. For those looking for a unique twist, other bungee jumping locations, such as the Grosser Sattel, offer beautiful views of the surrounding mountains and valleys, enhancing the overall experience.

In addition to paragliding and bungee jumping, Switzerland is a hub for a wide range of other adventure sports that cater to thrill-seekers. White-water rafting is particularly popular, with rivers like the Aare and the Lauterbrunnen offering rapids that challenge both novices and experienced rafters alike. The excitement of navigating through turbulent waters while surrounded by stunning alpine scenery makes this an unforgettable adventure. Professional guides ensure safety while providing expert instruction, making it accessible for all skill levels.

For those seeking a different kind of thrill, canyoning presents an exciting challenge. This adventure sport involves navigating through canyons using a mix of swimming, climbing, and jumping into crystal-clear pools. The Säntis Valley and the Chli Schliere are popular destinations for canyoning, where participants can explore the dramatic rock formations and waterfalls of the Swiss landscape. This exhilarating experience connects adventurers with nature in a unique way, allowing them to witness the beauty of Switzerland from a different perspective.

Hiking and mountain biking also offer adventure enthusiasts plenty of opportunities to explore the stunning landscapes of Switzerland. Trails range from leisurely walks along tranquil lakes to challenging climbs up steep mountain paths. The Zermatt region, for example, is renowned for its breathtaking hiking routes, which lead to breathtaking views of the Matterhorn. Mountain biking trails, such as those found in the Jungfrau region, provide adrenaline-fueled rides through picturesque landscapes, combining the thrill of speed with the beauty of nature.

Caving is yet another adventure to consider while in Switzerland. Exploring the country's vast network of caves, such as the Hölloch Cave, offers a unique opportunity to discover underground formations, including stunning stalactites and stalagmites. Guided tours often include spelunking and other activities, allowing participants to experience the mysterious beauty of the subterranean world.

Switzerland's diverse landscapes and commitment to adventure sports make it a premier destination for thrill-seekers. Whether soaring through the air while paragliding, plunging into the depths during a bungee jump, navigating wild rivers while rafting, or exploring canyons, visitors are sure to find an adventure that will satisfy their cravings for excitement. Each experience provides not just a rush of adrenaline but also a deeper appreciation for the natural beauty of the Swiss landscape, making these adventures unforgettable highlights of any trip to this stunning country.

Lake Activities: Boating, Swimming, and Fishing

The country is home to numerous lakes, each with its own unique charm and opportunities for outdoor recreation. Boating, swimming, and fishing are among the most popular activities that allow people to immerse themselves in the breathtaking natural beauty of the Swiss lakes.

Boating on Switzerland's lakes is a quintessential experience that combines relaxation with exploration. Many of the larger lakes, such as Lake Geneva, Lake Zurich, and Lake Lucerne, offer a variety of boating options, from leisurely paddleboats and rowboats to luxurious motor yachts and elegant sailboats. Visitors can rent boats or join guided tours to discover the picturesque shores, charming villages, and stunning mountain backdrops that characterize these iconic lakes.

Lake Geneva, for example, is famous for its scenic boat cruises that take passengers from city to city, showcasing the beauty of the surrounding landscape. The lake is dotted with quaint towns like Montreux and Évian-les-Bains, which can be easily accessed by boat. As the gentle waves lap against the hull, passengers can enjoy panoramic views of vineyards, historic châteaux, and the majestic Alps, making it a memorable way to experience the region. Lake Lucerne, known for its dramatic scenery and the surrounding mountains, offers a range of boat tours, including options to visit the nearby Mount Pilatus and Mount Rigi, which provide stunning views of the lake below.

Swimming in Switzerland's lakes is another refreshing way to enjoy the outdoors during the warmer months. Many lakes have designated swimming areas that are well-maintained and offer facilities such as changing rooms and showers. Lake Geneva and Lake Zurich, with their crystal-clear waters, are particularly popular for swimming, attracting both sunbathers and avid swimmers. The beaches along these lakes provide the perfect setting for a relaxing day by the water, with grassy areas for picnicking and sunbathing.

Swimmers can often be seen enjoying the cool waters while taking in the stunning views of the surrounding mountains and cities. The water temperature in Swiss lakes varies throughout the year, but during the summer months, it can reach pleasant levels, making swimming a popular activity for families and individuals seeking to cool off. For those looking for a more adventurous swimming experience, the option to dive into alpine lakes, such as Lake Brienz and Lake Thun, provides a unique opportunity to swim surrounded by dramatic mountain scenery.

Fishing is yet another cherished activity in Switzerland's lakes, attracting anglers from near and far. The country's lakes are home to a diverse range of fish species, including trout, perch, and whitefish, providing ample opportunities for both recreational and sport fishing. Anglers can enjoy fishing from the shore, in a boat, or even through ice fishing in the winter months on lakes that freeze over.

Many lakes offer fishing permits for visitors, and local regulations ensure sustainable practices to protect fish populations. Lake Geneva, with its abundant fish species and picturesque surroundings, is a popular destination for fishing enthusiasts. The tranquil environment and stunning views create a perfect backdrop for a day spent casting lines and waiting for the catch of the day. In addition to the thrill of catching fish, the experience of fishing in Switzerland's lakes offers a chance to connect with nature and enjoy the serenity of the alpine landscape.

Throughout the year, various festivals and events celebrate lake activities in Switzerland. For example, during the summer months, many towns and cities host regattas, sailing competitions, and other water sports events that showcase the region's maritime culture. These events not only highlight the beauty of the lakes but also bring together communities and visitors for shared experiences of outdoor fun and camaraderie.

The lake activities of boating, swimming, and fishing in Switzerland provide unforgettable experiences set against some of the most breathtaking landscapes in the world. Whether you're gliding across the water in a boat, taking a refreshing dip in a tranquil lake, or casting your line in search of the perfect catch, Switzerland's lakes offer a plethora of opportunities to enjoy the outdoors. The combination of stunning scenery, recreational activities, and the chance to connect with nature makes exploring Switzerland's lakes a must for anyone visiting this beautiful country.

Chapter 6. Food and Drink in Switzerland

Swiss Cheese and Chocolate: A Culinary Tour

Switzerland is a culinary paradise, renowned globally for its exquisite cheese and chocolate. These two iconic products are not merely food items; they represent a significant part of Swiss culture and tradition, offering a rich history and diverse flavors that entice food enthusiasts from around the world.

Swiss cheese is celebrated for its quality and variety, with over 450 distinct types produced throughout the country. The most famous of these is Emmental cheese, known for its characteristic holes and nutty flavor. Originating from the Emmental region, this cheese is a staple in Swiss cuisine and is often used in traditional dishes like fondue and raclette. Fondue, in particular, is a beloved Swiss tradition, where melted cheese is served in a communal pot, allowing diners to dip pieces of bread into the gooey goodness. The combination of Emmental with Gruyère cheese, another Swiss classic known for its smooth texture and slightly sweet flavor, creates a delightful harmony that is a must-try when visiting Switzerland.

Another notable cheese is Raclette, which is both a type of cheese and a cooking style. The name comes from the French word "racler," meaning to scrape. Traditionally, a wheel of raclette cheese is heated until it melts, and the gooey cheese is then scraped off onto boiled potatoes, pickles, and cured meats. This communal meal is perfect for gatherings, embodying the spirit of Swiss hospitality.

Tilsitand Appenzeller are additional Swiss cheeses worth exploring. Tilsit, with its tangy flavor, is perfect for sandwiches or as part of a cheese platter, while Appenzeller, characterized by its strong aroma and spicy flavor, is often used in cooking, particularly in fondue recipes.

The art of cheese-making in Switzerland dates back centuries, with techniques handed down through generations. Many cheesemakers continue to use traditional methods, ensuring the quality and authenticity of their products. Travelers can visit cheese dairies in various regions, such as the Swiss Alps, where they can witness the cheese-making process firsthand and sample fresh products. These tours often include tastings, allowing visitors to savor the distinct flavors of regional cheeses, often accompanied by a glass of Swiss wine or local bread.

While Swiss cheese holds a prominent place in the culinary landscape, Swiss chocolate is equally celebrated for its richness and craftsmanship. Switzerland is home to some of the world's most renowned chocolate brands, including Lindt, Toblerone, and Cailler, each offering a unique taste experience. Swiss chocolate is characterized by its smooth texture and high cocoa content, a result of meticulous production methods and the use of high-quality ingredients.

The origins of Swiss chocolate can be traced back to the 19th century when innovative chocolatiers began refining the chocolate-making process. The invention of the conching machine by Rudolf Lindt revolutionized chocolate production, creating a velvety smooth texture that is now synonymous with Swiss chocolate. This technique involves continuously mixing and aerating the chocolate to enhance its flavor and consistency.

Visitors to Switzerland can embark on a culinary tour dedicated to chocolate, exploring the country's chocolate factories and artisanal shops. These tours often include tastings of various chocolate varieties, from rich dark chocolate to creamy milk chocolate, and even unique flavors infused with spices, herbs, or fruit. Many chocolate makers also offer workshops where participants can try their hand at making their own chocolate, providing a hands-on experience that deepens their appreciation for this delectable treat.

One of the most iconic chocolate experiences in Switzerland is sampling the famous Toblerone, a triangular chocolate bar filled with nougat, almonds, and honey. Its distinctive shape and packaging make it a popular souvenir for travelers, while the rich flavors make it a delicious indulgence.

In addition to cheese and chocolate, Switzerland offers a wide range of culinary delights that complement these iconic products. Traditional Swiss cuisine features hearty dishes such as rösti, a potato dish similar to hash browns, and zopf, a braided bread often enjoyed on Sundays. These dishes pair wonderfully with Swiss cheese, creating a satisfying dining experience.

Swiss wine, particularly from regions such as Lavaux and Valais, also enhances the culinary journey. The country produces a variety of excellent white wines, primarily from the Chasselas grape, which pairs beautifully with cheese, making for an exquisite tasting experience.

A culinary tour of Switzerland centered around its cheese and chocolate offers a delightful exploration of the country's rich culinary heritage. From the traditional cheese-making processes in the Swiss Alps to the art of chocolate crafting in charming chocolateries, visitors are treated to a sensory experience that highlights the quality and passion behind these beloved Swiss products. Whether indulging in a warm cheese fondue or savoring a piece of artisanal chocolate, the flavors of Switzerland are sure to leave a lasting impression on every traveler.

Local Dishes: Fondue, Raclette, and More

Among the most iconic local dishes are fondue and raclette, both of which showcase Switzerland's rich dairy heritage and the communal spirit of its dining culture. These dishes reflect the rustic charm and traditions of

Swiss cuisine, making them essential experiences for any visitor.

Fondue, perhaps the most famous Swiss dish, consists of melted cheese served in a communal pot, known as a caquelon, over a small flame to keep it warm. Traditionally, a blend of cheeses such as Gruyère and Emmental is used, giving the dish a rich, creamy flavor with a slightly nutty undertone. The preparation of fondue is a social event in itself; diners dip pieces of crusty bread into the melted cheese using long forks, often accompanied by white wine, which enhances the flavor and helps keep the cheese smooth. The communal nature of fondue fosters a sense of togetherness, making it a popular choice for gatherings and celebrations.

Raclette is another beloved Swiss dish that revolves around the melting of cheese, but it differs from fondue in its presentation and preparation. Raclette cheese is heated until it becomes gooey and is then scraped onto boiled potatoes, pickles, and cured meats. Traditionally, the cheese is melted over an open fire, but in modern settings, specialized raclette grills allow diners to melt individual portions at their tables. The combination of the rich, melted cheese with the earthy flavors of the potatoes and the tangy pickles creates a comforting and satisfying meal. Like fondue, raclette is often enjoyed in a communal setting, encouraging sharing and conversation among diners.

Beyond fondue and raclette, Swiss cuisine offers a variety of other local dishes that highlight the country's agricultural bounty and culinary traditions. One such dish is rösti, a simple yet delicious potato dish that resembles a thick pancake. Rösti is made by grating potatoes, then frying or baking them until golden and crispy. Originally a breakfast staple in the German-speaking regions, rösti has become popular throughout Switzerland and is often served as a side dish alongside meats or as a base for toppings such as poached eggs, cheese, or vegetables.

Another notable dish is Zürcher Geschnetzeltes, a specialty from Zurich that consists of thinly sliced veal cooked in a creamy white wine and mushroom sauce. Traditionally served with rösti, this dish exemplifies the Swiss love for hearty and comforting meals. The combination of tender meat and rich sauce, alongside the crispy potatoes, makes it a favorite among locals and visitors alike.

For those with a sweet tooth, Swiss pastries and desserts are not to be missed. One of the most famous is the chocolate cake known as Sachertorte, which is a rich, dense chocolate cake typically filled with apricot jam and topped with dark chocolate icing. While its origins are linked to Austria, the Swiss have embraced and adapted this dessert, often serving it with a dollop of whipped cream. Additionally, Swiss meringues, light and airy confections made from whipped egg whites and sugar, are a popular treat, especially when paired with fresh berries or fruit compote.

As one traverses the diverse regions of Switzerland, each area offers its own specialties influenced by local ingredients and traditions. In the Italian-speaking region of Ticino, for instance, polenta is a staple, often served with braised meats or sautéed vegetables. The French-speaking areas of Switzerland offer dishes like fondue moitié-moitié, a variation of traditional fondue made with a blend of Gruyère and Fribourg cheese, and coq au vin, which reflects the culinary influences of neighboring France.

Seasonal and regional ingredients play a significant role in Swiss cuisine. During the summer, fresh vegetables, herbs, and berries take center stage, while the winter months highlight hearty root vegetables, game meats, and preserved foods. Local markets throughout the country provide an abundance of fresh produce, cheeses, and meats, encouraging the use of high-quality ingredients in traditional recipes.

The Swiss take great pride in their culinary heritage, and food is often at the heart of social gatherings and celebrations. Whether enjoyed in cozy mountain huts, upscale restaurants, or at family gatherings, local dishes like fondue and raclette embody the spirit of Swiss hospitality and the country's appreciation for good food. Experiencing these iconic dishes is not only a treat for the palate but also a glimpse into the rich cultural tapestry that defines Switzerland. Visitors are encouraged to partake in the communal experience of these meals, savoring the flavors and the sense of togetherness that comes with sharing food.

Top Swiss Wineries and Vineyards

Switzerland, although often overshadowed by its neighboring countries in the realm of wine production, boasts a rich viticultural heritage that reflects its unique geography and climate. With its diverse terroirs and a wide range of grape varieties, Swiss wineries and vineyards produce exceptional wines that are increasingly gaining recognition on the global stage.

The vineyards of Switzerland are primarily situated in the regions of Vaud, Valais, Geneva, and Neuchâtel. The Valais region, located in the Rhône Valley, is the largest wine-producing area in the country. Here, the combination of sun-soaked slopes, the Rhone River, and the stunning backdrop of the Alps creates an ideal environment for viticulture. The region is known for its indigenous grape varieties, such as Petite Arvine, Amigne, and Cornalin, as well as international varieties like Chardonnay and Merlot. One of the most renowned wineries in Valais is Domaine des Muses, known for its high-quality white wines made from local grapes that showcase the unique characteristics of the region.

Moving to the Vaud region, which encompasses the picturesque Lavaux vineyards, recognized as a UNESCO World Heritage site, visitors can explore terraced vineyards that slope dramatically down to Lake Geneva. This region is famous for its Chasselas grape, which produces crisp, mineral-driven white wines that pair beautifully with local cuisine. The Domaine Bovy is a standout winery in Lavaux, offering a selection of organic wines and stunning views of the lake and mountains. Wine lovers can enjoy tastings on-site while soaking in the breathtaking scenery that surrounds them.

In the Geneva region, the wine culture is thriving, with numerous wineries producing high-quality wines in a relatively small area. The Domaine La Colombe is a notable producer, celebrated for its commitment to sustainable practices and the production of elegant wines, including both red and white varieties. The Geneva vineyards are often characterized by their use of traditional methods, and visitors to the area can partake in guided tours and tastings that showcase the craftsmanship behind each bottle.

The Neuchâtel region, located near the shores of Lake Neuchâtel, is known for its charming vineyards and picturesque landscapes. The wineries here focus on both red and white varieties, with Pinot Noir and Chasselas being the most prominent. Domaine de la Tille is a noteworthy winery in Neuchâtel, known for its dedication to organic farming and the production of wines that express the local terroir. Visitors can explore the vineyard's beautiful grounds and enjoy tastings that highlight the distinctive flavors of the region.

Switzerland's commitment to sustainable viticulture is evident across its wineries, with many producers adopting organic and biodynamic practices to ensure the health of the vines and the environment. This dedication to sustainability not only contributes to the quality of the wines but also enhances the overall experience for visitors who are increasingly interested in eco-friendly practices.

In addition to the well-known regions, there are also hidden gems scattered throughout the country. The Appenzell region, with its rolling hills and quaint villages, produces delightful wines that are lesser-known but worth exploring. Here, small family-owned wineries like Weinbau Wenk produce limited quantities of handcrafted wines that reflect the unique terroir of the region.

Visiting Swiss wineries often involves much more than just tasting wine. Many vineyards offer guided tours, providing insight into the winemaking process and the history of the region. Visitors can stroll through the vineyards, learning about the different grape varieties, the importance of terroir, and the sustainable practices employed by the winemakers. Additionally, many wineries feature charming restaurants or picnic areas where guests can enjoy local delicacies paired with the wines produced on-site.

Wine festivals are also a vibrant part of Swiss culture, with events celebrating the harvest and the art of winemaking throughout the year. These festivals provide an opportunity for visitors to sample a wide range of wines, meet local winemakers, and immerse themselves in the lively atmosphere that surrounds Swiss wine culture.

Switzerland's wineries and vineyards offer a unique and enriching experience for wine lovers and travelers alike. With their breathtaking landscapes, commitment to sustainability, and a diverse array of high-quality wines, these vineyards are a testament to the country's rich viticultural heritage. Whether exploring the terraced vineyards of Lavaux, tasting the elegant wines of Geneva, or discovering hidden gems in the Appenzell region, visitors to Swiss wineries are sure to enjoy a memorable and flavorful journey through the heart of Swiss wine country.

Where to Eat: Best Restaurants, Cafes, and Markets

In major cities like Zurich, Geneva, and Basel, fine dining establishments showcase the best of Swiss cuisine and international fare. Restaurants such as Restaurant Pavillon in Zurich, located in the Baur Au Lac Hotel, offer an exquisite dining experience with Michelin-starred dishes crafted from seasonal ingredients. The elegant atmosphere and stunning views of Lake Zurich enhance the overall experience, making it a perfect choice for special occasions. In Geneva, the Michelin-starred restaurant Bayview serves contemporary cuisine with a focus on fresh, local products, all while offering spectacular views of Lake Geneva and the Alps. The combination of creative dishes and exceptional service makes these restaurants stand out among the culinary offerings.

For those seeking a more casual dining experience, Switzerland boasts numerous traditional Swiss restaurants. These eateries often serve iconic dishes such as fondue, raclette, and rösti. In the picturesque town of Zermatt, restaurants like Restaurant Whymper-Stube invite visitors to indulge in authentic Swiss fondue, allowing them to immerse themselves in the local culinary culture. Similarly, in Lausanne, Café de Grancy is a popular spot that serves delicious rösti along with a selection of local wines in a warm and inviting atmosphere.

Cafés are an integral part of Swiss culture, providing the perfect setting for a leisurely afternoon or a quick snack. In cities like Zurich, the historic Café Schober is famous for its stunning interior and delightful pastries. The café's cakes and chocolates are a must-try, particularly the rich and decadent Swiss chocolate cake. In Geneva, Café de la Paix offers a charming ambiance and a menu featuring freshly brewed coffee, delicious pastries, and light lunch options. This café is an ideal spot for people-watching and enjoying the local atmosphere.

Street food is also gaining popularity in Switzerland, especially in urban areas where food markets and stalls provide a taste of local flavors. Markets like the Helvetiaplatz Market in Zurich and the Plainpalais Flea Market in Geneva feature a variety of food vendors offering everything from freshly made pretzels and sausages to exotic international dishes. Visitors can sample local specialties like Zürcher Geschnetzeltes, a creamy veal dish, or try regional cheeses and cured meats. The vibrant atmosphere of these markets makes them a great place to enjoy a casual meal and experience the local community.

Switzerland's multicultural environment means visitors can enjoy a plethora of international cuisines. In Geneva, neighborhoods like Carouge are known for their diverse dining options, featuring Italian, Moroccan, and Asian restaurants. The city's vibrant food scene reflects the influences of its cosmopolitan population. In Zurich, the trendy district of Kreis 5 is home to various eateries, including hip cafés and modern bistros serving everything from gourmet burgers to vegan dishes.

Food festivals and events are also an excellent opportunity to explore Swiss culinary delights. Events like the Montreux Jazz Festival not only feature music but also offer a chance to taste local foods from various vendors. Similarly, the Fête de la Musique in Geneva is a lively celebration of music and culture, where food stalls showcase regional specialties and artisanal products.

Switzerland is also home to several bustling food markets that celebrate local produce and artisanal goods. The Zürich Hauptbahnhof's Market Hall features an array of stalls selling fresh fruits, vegetables, cheeses, meats, and baked goods, making it an ideal spot for picking up local specialties or enjoying a quick bite. In Lausanne, the Ouchy Promenade Market offers a scenic location to enjoy local products, including seasonal fruits, flowers, and handmade crafts.

The dining scene in Switzerland reflects the country's rich culinary heritage and contemporary influences. From fine dining to cozy cafés and vibrant markets, there is no shortage of options for those looking to indulge in the flavors of Switzerland. Whether savoring traditional dishes or exploring international cuisine, visitors will find that the Swiss culinary landscape offers a delightful and memorable experience.

Chapter 7. Luxury Travel in Switzerland

High-End Resorts and Spas

The Swiss Alps are home to some of the most exclusive resorts in the world, attracting discerning guests with their stunning mountain views and world-class amenities. One such resort is located in Zermatt, a car-free village that boasts the iconic Matterhorn as its backdrop. The area is renowned for its luxurious chalets and five-star hotels, many of which feature gourmet restaurants, sumptuous spas, and direct access to some of the best skiing in the world. Guests can enjoy personalized services, from private ski instructors to spa treatments using locally sourced products, all while basking in the tranquil atmosphere of the mountains.

In St. Moritz, known for its status as a winter playground for the elite, luxury resorts offer a unique blend of opulence and adventure. The town is famous for hosting the Winter Olympics twice, and its hotels reflect this legacy of prestige. Visitors can enjoy lavish accommodations with stunning views of the lake and surrounding peaks, as well as a variety of winter sports, fine dining experiences, and exclusive shopping opportunities. The local spas provide a range of treatments that combine traditional Swiss wellness practices with modern techniques, ensuring guests leave feeling rejuvenated and pampered.

Another gem in the Swiss luxury landscape is the resort town of Gstaad, which attracts celebrities and high-profile guests from around the globe. The luxurious chalets and upscale hotels here are characterized by their traditional wooden architecture and breathtaking alpine settings. Visitors can engage in activities such as skiing, snowboarding, and hiking during the summer months, all while enjoying the impeccable service offered at the region's spas. Many resorts feature wellness centers that provide holistic treatments, wellness programs, and relaxation areas that invite guests to unwind and recharge.

Lake Geneva is also a prime location for high-end resorts, where visitors can enjoy both stunning lake views and the grandeur of the Alps. The luxury hotels in cities like Montreux and Lausanne offer an elegant blend of Swiss hospitality and modern comforts. These establishments often include gourmet dining options that highlight regional cuisine, along with extensive wellness facilities that may include thermal baths, saunas, and relaxation lounges. The peaceful lakeside setting provides an idyllic backdrop for spa treatments that incorporate local traditions, such as vinotherapy, which uses the beneficial properties of grapes to nourish the skin.

The emphasis on wellness is a significant aspect of Switzerland's high-end resorts. Many properties are equipped with state-of-the-art spas that focus on holistic health and relaxation. Treatments may range from massages and facials to thermal baths and aromatherapy sessions, all designed to provide guests with an immersive experience that revitalizes both body and mind. The use of natural, high-quality products is common, reflecting the country's commitment to sustainability and organic wellness.

Some resorts offer unique wellness experiences inspired by the surrounding nature. Guests might participate in outdoor yoga sessions with stunning mountain views, guided nature walks, or meditation classes in serene gardens. These experiences not only enhance physical well-being but also foster a deeper connection to the breathtaking Swiss landscape.

For those seeking culinary excellence, many high-end resorts feature acclaimed restaurants helmed by renowned chefs. Guests can indulge in gourmet meals that showcase local ingredients and traditional Swiss flavors, paired with fine wines from the region. Dining at these establishments often becomes an event in itself, as many resorts offer exceptional ambiance and breathtaking views that elevate the entire experience.

Moreover, the service at Swiss high-end resorts is impeccable. Staff members are trained to anticipate guests' needs and provide personalized experiences that cater to individual preferences. From arranging private transportation to planning exclusive excursions, these resorts ensure that every aspect of a guest's stay is seamless and memorable.

High-end resorts and spas in Switzerland provide an unparalleled experience for travelers seeking luxury, relaxation, and adventure. Set against stunning backdrops of mountains and lakes, these establishments offer a perfect blend of world-class accommodations, exceptional service, and rejuvenating wellness treatments. Whether indulging in gourmet cuisine, enjoying exclusive spa experiences, or exploring the majestic Swiss landscape, visitors to these luxurious resorts will find themselves immersed in the beauty and elegance that define Switzerland.

Scenic Train Rides (Bernina Express, Glacier Express)

The Bernina Express is a remarkable journey that takes passengers from Chur, the oldest city in Switzerland, to Tirano, a small town in Italy. This route is celebrated for its spectacular views of the Swiss Alps, with the train climbing to an impressive altitude of over 2,253 meters at the Bernina Pass. The journey spans approximately four hours and covers 60 kilometers, weaving through breathtaking landscapes that include glaciers, emerald lakes, and charming mountain villages.

One of the highlights of the Bernina Express is the section that passes over the iconic Brusio Spiral Viaduct, an engineering marvel that allows the train to gain altitude in a remarkably graceful manner. This circular bridge not only serves a practical purpose but also offers a unique visual experience, as the train spirals around the track in a dramatic twist.

As the train continues its ascent, passengers are treated to sweeping panoramas of the surrounding mountains, including the impressive Piz Bernina, which stands as a sentinel over the landscape. The route also passes through the charming village of St. Moritz, a famous winter resort known for its luxury and outdoor activities. The contrast between the lush green valleys and the stark white glaciers creates a stunning visual tapestry, making every moment on the train feel like a postcard come to life.

The Glacier Express, often dubbed the "slowest express train in the world," offers a different but equally mesmerizing experience. It connects Zermatt, located at the base of the iconic Matterhorn, to St. Moritz, winding through some of the most spectacular landscapes in the Swiss Alps. The journey takes approximately eight hours and covers 291 kilometers, with the train traversing 91 tunnels and crossing 291 bridges along the way.

What sets the Glacier Express apart is its ability to offer breathtaking views from panoramic windows that provide an unobstructed view of the surrounding scenery. The train's design includes large glass domes, allowing passengers to feel fully immersed in the alpine environment. As the train makes its way through dramatic gorges, lush valleys, and picturesque villages, travelers can admire the stunning contrasts of the landscape, from deep blue skies to shimmering lakes and towering peaks.

One of the most notable sections of the Glacier Express is the ascent to the Oberalp Pass, which is the highest point of the journey at an altitude of 2,033 meters. Here, passengers can experience the exhilarating transition from lush valleys to the stark beauty of the alpine environment, where snow-capped peaks and serene glacial landscapes dominate the horizon.

The train also passes through the charming village of Andermatt, which serves as a gateway to the stunning landscapes of the Gotthard region. Travelers can enjoy views of the Rhone Glacier, the source of the River Rhone, and take in the majestic scenery that has inspired countless artists and adventurers alike.

Both the Bernina Express and the Glacier Express highlight Switzerland's commitment to maintaining an efficient and sustainable transportation system while also showcasing the country's natural beauty. The trains are equipped with comfortable seating, dining options, and knowledgeable staff who provide commentary on the sights along the route, enhancing the overall experience for travelers.

Traveling on these scenic train rides allows visitors to unwind and appreciate the tranquility of the Swiss landscape. With no need to navigate winding mountain roads, passengers can simply relax and enjoy the ride, taking in the panoramic views that change with every curve of the track. Whether witnessing the breathtaking majesty of the Alps, the tranquil beauty of alpine lakes, or the charm of historic villages, these train journeys offer an unforgettable way to experience Switzerland's stunning scenery.

The Bernina Express and the Glacier Express are more than just modes of transportation; they are journeys that immerse travelers in the natural beauty and cultural richness of Switzerland. Each ride is a unique experience, allowing passengers to connect with the landscape in a way that is both relaxing and exhilarating, making these scenic train rides essential components of any Swiss travel itinerary.

Exclusive Shopping Districts in Zurich and Geneva

Zurich and Geneva, the two largest cities in Switzerland, are renowned not only for their picturesque landscapes and cultural offerings but also for their exclusive shopping districts. These urban areas showcase luxury brands, high-end boutiques, and unique Swiss craftsmanship, making them premier destinations for discerning shoppers.

In Zurich, Bahnhofstrasse is arguably one of the most famous shopping streets in the world. This tree-lined boulevard stretches from the main train station to Lake Zurich and is renowned for its concentration of luxury shops and department stores. As one walks along Bahnhofstrasse, one encounters an impressive array of designer boutiques, including names like Louis Vuitton, Chanel, and Gucci, alongside Swiss watchmakers such as Rolex and Patek Philippe. The street's elegance is further enhanced by its vibrant atmosphere, characterized by bustling cafes and art installations that contribute to the overall shopping experience.

Within Bahnhofstrasse, luxury department stores like Jelmoli and Globus stand out. Jelmoli offers a wide range of high-end fashion, beauty products, and gourmet food, making it a one-stop destination for luxury shopping. The beautifully curated displays and personalized service make each visit a unique experience. Globus, on the other hand, combines fashion with an upscale grocery experience, featuring an extensive food section that showcases the best of Swiss and international delicacies.

Just off Bahnhofstrasse, the Zurich Old Town, or Altstadt, offers a different shopping experience. Here, cobblestone streets are lined with charming boutiques, artisanal shops, and independent designers. The area retains a historic charm that contrasts with the sleek modernity of Bahnhofstrasse, creating a delightful ambiance for leisurely exploration. Visitors can discover unique Swiss products, handcrafted jewelry, and contemporary fashion in these smaller shops, providing a more personalized shopping experience.

In Geneva, the Rue du Rhône serves as the city's premier shopping destination. This elegant street is home to numerous luxury brands and flagship stores, attracting both local and international clientele. As one strolls down Rue du Rhône, it becomes evident why Geneva is often referred to as the "capital of luxury." High-end jewelry stores, including the likes of Chopard and Piaget, sit alongside renowned fashion houses such as Dior and Hermès. The allure of these prestigious brands draws shoppers seeking exclusive items and impeccable craftsmanship.

Another notable feature of Rue du Rhône is its proximity to the scenic Lake Geneva. This stunning backdrop enhances the shopping experience, allowing visitors to enjoy beautiful views while exploring the shops. The area is also home to chic cafes and restaurants, offering a perfect spot to relax after a day of shopping.

While Rue du Rhône focuses heavily on luxury brands, Geneva's Carouge district provides a charming alternative. Known for its artistic vibe, Carouge features an array of independent boutiques, art galleries, and artisan workshops. This district, with its bohemian atmosphere and colorful buildings, offers a delightful contrast to the high-end shopping found on Rue du Rhône. Shoppers can explore local craftsmanship, including handmade jewelry, unique clothing, and beautiful home decor. The district hosts regular artisan markets and cultural events, enhancing its appeal as a creative hub.

Both Zurich and Geneva also offer exclusive shopping experiences through various luxury shopping centers. In Zurich, the Sihlcity complex combines shopping with entertainment, featuring a range of luxury brands alongside cinemas and dining options. This modern shopping center creates a lively environment where visitors can enjoy both retail therapy and leisure activities.

In Geneva, the Balexert shopping center is another destination that caters to high-end shoppers. It hosts a selection of luxury boutiques and international brands, along with gourmet food options, making it a convenient stop for those seeking an upscale shopping experience in a more relaxed environment.

The overall shopping experience in Zurich and Geneva is marked by a commitment to quality, luxury, and craftsmanship. Both cities embody the Swiss ethos of precision and excellence, evident in the products offered in their exclusive shopping districts. Whether one is exploring the glamorous storefronts of Bahnhofstrasse and Rue du Rhône or discovering hidden gems in the

Old Town and Carouge, the shopping experience in these cities is sure to leave a lasting impression. The combination of stunning surroundings, premium products, and exceptional service creates a shopping environment that is both enjoyable and memorable, making Zurich and Geneva must-visit destinations for luxury enthusiasts and fashion lovers alike.

Chapter 8. Budget Travel Tips

Affordable Accommodations

Finding affordable accommodations in Switzerland can enhance your travel experience without breaking the bank. While the country is known for its high standard of living and luxury offerings, there are plenty of budget-friendly options available that cater to various tastes and preferences.

Hostels are a popular choice for budget travelers, providing not only economical lodging but also a vibrant social atmosphere. Many Swiss cities have hostels that are centrally located, making it easy to explore the local attractions. These hostels often offer dormitory-style rooms as well as private rooms, giving guests flexibility depending on their comfort and budget needs. Some notable hostels, such as the Youth Hostels in Zurich and Geneva, are well-rated for their cleanliness and facilities, including communal kitchens and lounges. Staying in a hostel can also provide opportunities to meet fellow travelers and exchange tips about exploring Switzerland.

For those seeking a more local experience, guesthouses and bed-and-breakfasts offer charming and affordable alternatives to hotels. These accommodations are often run by locals who can provide insider tips about the area and may even serve homemade breakfast featuring regional specialties. Staying in a guesthouse can add a personal touch to your trip and help you connect with the culture of the area. Many guesthouses are located in picturesque rural settings, allowing guests to experience Switzerland's stunning landscapes up close.

Camping is another great option for travelers looking to save money while immersing themselves in nature. Switzerland has an extensive network of campsites, many of which are situated near lakes, rivers, or mountain trails. Campsites provide essential facilities like restrooms, showers, and cooking areas, making them a comfortable choice for those who enjoy the outdoors. In summer, camping allows visitors to experience the breathtaking scenery of the Swiss Alps and enjoy activities such as hiking, cycling, and swimming in pristine lakes. Some campsites even offer cabins or glamping options for those who prefer a little more comfort while still enjoying the camping experience.

Airbnb and similar vacation rental platforms have gained popularity in recent years, offering affordable alternatives to traditional hotels. Renting a room or an entire apartment can be a cost-effective way to stay in prime locations without paying hotel prices. Many listings are available in charming neighborhoods, allowing travelers to experience life like a local. Additionally, having access to a kitchen can help save money on dining out, as you can prepare your own meals using fresh ingredients from local markets.

In addition to these options, many cities in Switzerland offer budget hotels and chain accommodations that provide comfort and convenience at lower prices. These establishments may not have the character of a boutique hotel or guesthouse, but they offer essential amenities such as free Wi-Fi, breakfast, and sometimes even parking. Booking in advance or searching for deals during off-peak seasons can yield significant savings, making it possible to find comfortable lodging without overspending.

Staying with locals through platforms like Couchsurfing can also be an intriguing way to save money while experiencing Swiss hospitality firsthand. This service connects travelers with local hosts willing to offer free accommodation in exchange for cultural exchange or simply as a way to meet new people. While the experience varies, it can lead to memorable interactions and valuable insights into local customs and attractions.

For those traveling in groups or families, renting a vacation home or chalet can provide affordable accommodations while allowing everyone to stay together. Many homes come equipped with kitchens and communal spaces, making it a great option for shared meals and quality time. This arrangement can also be more economical than booking multiple hotel rooms, especially for longer stays.

Affordable accommodations in Switzerland are plentiful and varied, ensuring that travelers can find a suitable option to fit their budget. Whether you choose a hostel, guesthouse, campsite, vacation rental, or budget hotel, there are many ways to enjoy Switzerland's beauty and culture without overspending. With careful planning and research, you can experience the charm of this stunning country while keeping your travel expenses manageable.

Money-Saving Tips for Swiss Travel

Traveling in Switzerland can be expensive, but with some thoughtful planning and smart strategies, you can significantly reduce costs and make the most of your trip. There are several ways to save money on transportation, food, activities, and accommodation without compromising your experience.

One of the most effective ways to save money in Switzerland is by taking advantage of the country's excellent public transportation system. The Swiss Travel Pass is a great option for tourists, offering unlimited travel on trains, buses, and boats throughout the country for a set number of days. The pass also provides free or discounted entry to many museums and attractions, making it an excellent value for those who plan to explore different regions. Booking your tickets in advance can often lead to substantial discounts, especially if you opt for saver fares or off-peak travel times. Trains in Switzerland are reliable, clean, and offer scenic journeys, so opting for public transport over car rentals can be both economical and enjoyable.

If you do prefer to drive, renting a car outside of Switzerland, particularly in neighboring countries like Germany or France, can often be cheaper. It's important to note that Switzerland requires a vignette, or road tax sticker, for driving on highways, which is often included in car rentals. However, driving is only recommended if you plan to visit remote areas that are less accessible by train, as parking and fuel costs in Switzerland can be high.

Accommodation is another area where you can cut costs. Consider staying in hostels, guesthouses, or budget hotels, which tend to offer better rates than high-end hotels. Many hostels in Switzerland are modern and comfortable, providing shared kitchen facilities where you can prepare your own meals. Booking accommodations in advance or traveling during the off-peak seasons, such as spring or fall, can also lead to lower rates. Additionally, vacation rentals through platforms like Airbnb can offer a cost-effective alternative to hotels, especially if you're traveling with a group and can share expenses.

Food and dining can quickly add up in Switzerland, but there are several ways to enjoy the local cuisine without overspending. One of the best tips is to shop at local supermarkets, such as Migros or Coop, which offer a wide variety of affordable groceries, ready-made meals, and snacks. Many supermarkets also have salad bars, hot meals, and sandwiches that make for inexpensive and delicious on-the-go meals. Cooking your own meals, especially if you have access to a kitchen in a vacation rental or hostel, is a great way to save money while still enjoying local ingredients.

When dining out, consider opting for lunch instead of dinner, as many restaurants offer cheaper set menus during lunchtime. In addition, self-service cafeterias like those found in department stores or at major train stations often serve good quality meals at lower prices. Street food, such as sausages, pretzels, or cheese-based dishes like raclette and fondue, is also widely available and can be a more affordable way to experience traditional Swiss flavors.

For sightseeing and activities, there are plenty of free or low-cost options that allow you to experience the beauty of Switzerland without breaking the bank. Many of Switzerland's most stunning attractions, such as its mountains, lakes, and hiking trails, are free to enjoy. Exploring cities on foot or by bike is a great way to take in the scenery and discover hidden gems without spending money. Museums and cultural attractions often offer free entry on specific days or discounted rates with a Swiss Travel Pass, so it's worth researching your options in advance.

If you're an avid hiker or nature lover, Switzerland is a paradise of free outdoor activities. The country has an extensive network of well-marked hiking trails, ranging from easy walks around lakes to challenging alpine treks. Many of these trails offer breathtaking views of the Swiss Alps, and you can explore them at no cost. In winter, cross-country skiing and snowshoeing are often more affordable alternatives to downhill skiing, and you can rent equipment for a reasonable price.

Switzerland is also home to a variety of free festivals, markets, and public events throughout the year. In cities like Zurich, Geneva, and Basel, you can often find street performances, concerts, and art exhibitions that are open to the public. Seasonal markets, particularly during the holidays, offer a festive atmosphere and an opportunity to sample local foods and buy unique souvenirs without spending much money.

Planning and timing your activities can lead to significant savings. Many attractions and tours offer discounts if booked online in advance. Traveling during the shoulder seasons, such as late spring or early autumn, not only helps you avoid the crowds but can also lead to lower prices for accommodations, flights, and activities. By being flexible with your travel dates and taking advantage of deals, you can stretch your budget further and enjoy more of what Switzerland has to offer.

While Switzerland is known for its high costs, there are numerous ways to save money and still have a memorable experience. Whether through smart transportation choices, budget-friendly accommodations, or free outdoor activities, you can enjoy the beauty, culture, and charm of Switzerland without overspending. With a little planning and creativity, your Swiss adventure can be both affordable and unforgettable.

Budget-Friendly Eateries and Markets

Switzerland, while known for its high living costs, offers plenty of opportunities to eat well without stretching your budget. Budget-friendly eateries and markets are scattered throughout the country, providing a range of delicious and affordable dining options that allow travelers to experience local flavors while keeping costs down.

One of the best ways to enjoy affordable meals in Switzerland is to visit the many casual eateries and cafés that serve traditional Swiss fare at reasonable prices. These establishments often offer hearty dishes like rosti, a crispy potato pancake, or simple cheese fondue without the high prices found at more upscale restaurants. In cities like Zurich, Geneva, and Lucerne, you'll find cozy, family-run spots where locals dine, often offering daily specials or set menus that provide excellent value. Additionally, bakeries and sandwich shops are widespread, serving freshly baked bread, pastries, and affordable sandwiches made with local cheeses, meats, and seasonal ingredients.

Street food is another way to eat well on a budget in Switzerland. The country's cities and towns host a variety of street vendors and food stalls, particularly in busy areas and during festivals. Sausages, particularly the classic bratwurst, are popular street food items and can be found in most cities. Served with a side of mustard and crusty bread, they provide a filling and inexpensive meal on the go. In larger cities like Basel and Lausanne, food trucks and pop-up vendors also offer a range of international cuisine, from falafel and kebabs to Asian stir-fries and Italian-style pizzas. This diversity of options makes it easy to find affordable meals that suit different tastes.

Markets play a significant role in Switzerland's food culture and are excellent places to find budget-friendly eats. Farmers' markets, held weekly in most towns and cities, offer fresh, locally sourced produce, artisanal cheeses, cured meats, and baked goods. These markets are perfect for picking up ingredients to prepare your own meals, especially if you're staying in accommodations with kitchen facilities. Buying directly from local farmers and producers not only supports the regional economy but also gives you access to the highest quality ingredients at lower prices than grocery stores.

Some markets, like the Plainpalais Market in Geneva or the Oerlikon Market in Zurich, are especially well-known for their wide variety of products, ranging from fresh fruits and vegetables to ready-to-eat street food. Many stalls at these markets sell affordable snacks and meals, including savory tarts, grilled meats, and traditional Swiss pastries like Nusstorte (nut cake). Visiting a market is also an opportunity to interact with locals, learn more about Swiss food culture, and discover regional specialties.

For those looking to save even more on dining, supermarkets and grocery stores are essential stops. Chains like Migros, Coop, and Aldi offer ready-made meals, sandwiches, and salads at prices far below those of sit-down restaurants. Many supermarkets have deli sections with hot meals, where you can find everything from roast chicken to pasta dishes and soups, all at budget-friendly prices. Some larger branches of Migros and Coop even have in-store cafés where you can sit down for a simple, inexpensive meal. These grocery stores are also ideal for picking up snacks, drinks, and supplies for picnics, especially if you're planning to spend time outdoors or exploring Switzerland's stunning natural landscapes.

Self-catering is another great way to save on food costs while traveling in Switzerland. By purchasing ingredients at markets or supermarkets, you can prepare your own meals, which can be both cost-effective and enjoyable. Local cheeses, fresh bread, and seasonal produce are readily available, making it easy to put together a delicious Swiss-style picnic. Many parks, lakesides, and scenic viewpoints offer picnic areas, allowing you to enjoy your meal in a beautiful setting.

In addition to traditional Swiss food, Switzerland's multicultural population means that affordable international cuisine is widely available. In cities with diverse populations, such as Zurich and Basel, you'll find a variety of ethnic restaurants serving affordable dishes from countries like Turkey, India, and Thailand. These establishments often offer generous portions at reasonable prices, making them popular with both locals and travelers seeking a good meal without spending too much.

Switzerland also has a number of canteens and casual dining spots located in large department stores, such as Manor and Globus. These in-store cafeterias offer freshly prepared meals at lower prices than typical restaurants. The quality of food is generally high, with a selection of Swiss and international dishes, making them a great option for a quick and affordable lunch while shopping or sightseeing.

Budget-friendly eateries and markets are abundant in Switzerland, offering travelers a chance to enjoy local and international cuisine without overspending. From casual cafés and street food to vibrant markets and self-catering options, there are plenty of ways to experience the country's culinary diversity on a budget. By exploring these affordable dining options, you can savor the flavors of Switzerland while keeping your travel expenses under control.

Free Attractions and Activities

Switzerland, known for its breathtaking landscapes and cultural richness, offers plenty of free attractions and activities that allow travelers to experience the country without spending a fortune. Whether you're interested in nature, history, or local culture, there are numerous opportunities to explore Switzerland without opening your wallet.

One of the most accessible free activities in Switzerland is simply enjoying its stunning natural scenery. The country's numerous hiking trails are open to the public and allow you to experience the majestic beauty of the Swiss Alps, pristine lakes, and picturesque valleys. Popular hiking areas include the regions around Lake Geneva, the Bernese Oberland, and the Engadine Valley. These trails range from easy walks to more challenging routes, offering something for everyone. Along the way, you can take in panoramic views, breathe fresh mountain air, and appreciate the flora and fauna that thrive in Switzerland's diverse ecosystems. In winter, many areas also offer free access to snowshoe trails, allowing visitors to explore snowy landscapes without paying for ski passes.

Lakes and rivers across Switzerland provide another way to enjoy the country for free. Many of Switzerland's lakes, such as Lake Geneva, Lake Zurich, and Lake Lucerne, have public swimming areas where you can relax, swim, or have a picnic by the water. Some lakeside towns offer well-maintained promenades, perfect for leisurely strolls with incredible views of the surrounding mountains and landscapes. For those who enjoy a more active experience, you can walk or cycle around the lakes on well-marked trails, with many offering viewpoints and rest spots along the way. These lakeside areas are also great for spotting wildlife and enjoying Switzerland's serene natural beauty.

In Swiss cities, many cultural landmarks and historic sites are open to the public for free or have designated free entry days. For instance, walking through the old towns of cities like Bern, Zurich, and Geneva offers a fascinating glimpse into the country's medieval history. In Bern, the UNESCO World Heritage-listed old town is a beautifully preserved area with cobbled streets, charming fountains, and the iconic Zytglogge clock tower. Zurich's old town, known as Altstadt, is filled with narrow alleyways, historic churches, and medieval buildings, making it an excellent place for a self-guided walking tour.

Museums across Switzerland often offer free entry on certain days or have free permanent exhibitions. In Geneva, the International Red Cross and Red Crescent Museum provides free admission on the first Saturday of each month, giving visitors the chance to learn about the history and humanitarian efforts of the organization. The Swiss National Museum in Zurich also occasionally offers free access to its exhibits, which showcase Switzerland's cultural and historical heritage. Many smaller local museums, especially in rural areas, have free or donation-based entry, providing insights into regional traditions and crafts.

Art lovers will find many opportunities to enjoy Switzerland's vibrant art scene for free. Public art installations can be found throughout major cities, with sculptures, murals, and artistic landmarks dotting public squares and parks. In Zurich, for example, art lovers can visit the outdoor exhibition at the city's Sculpture Park, where works by renowned Swiss and international artists are on display. Geneva also features numerous outdoor sculptures and fountains that reflect the city's creative spirit.

Switzerland's parks and gardens are another source of free enjoyment. The Botanical Garden in Zurich, located on the university campus, is home to a wide variety of plants from around the world and is free to visit year-round. Similarly, the Geneva Botanical Gardens offer beautiful walking paths among themed gardens and greenhouses, where you can learn about plant species from different climates. Parks such as the English Garden in Geneva or Parc des Bastions, also in Geneva, provide serene spaces for relaxation and outdoor activities, and often host free events or festivals throughout the year.

Switzerland's vibrant street festivals and local events offer free entertainment and a chance to experience Swiss culture. Many towns and cities host festivals celebrating everything from music to regional traditions, with open-air performances, markets, and parades. In Zurich, the annual Street Parade, one of the largest electronic music festivals in the world, is a free event that attracts thousands of visitors. Likewise, the Montreux Jazz Festival, while ticketed for indoor performances, offers many free concerts and activities along the Lake Geneva shoreline.

Seasonal markets are another fantastic way to experience local culture for free. Christmas markets in cities like Basel, Lucerne, and Montreux fill the air with festive cheer and offer a delightful browsing experience. Visitors can wander among the stalls, enjoy the holiday lights, and soak in the seasonal atmosphere without necessarily making any purchases. In the summer, farmers' markets are common across Swiss towns, where you can explore local produce, handcrafted goods, and traditional Swiss foods, all while enjoying the lively market ambiance.

Overall, Switzerland's abundant natural beauty, rich cultural heritage, and well-preserved public spaces provide numerous opportunities for free activities and attractions. Whether exploring picturesque hiking trails, wandering through historic city centers, or immersing yourself in local festivals and markets, there are countless ways to experience the best of Switzerland on a budget.

Chapter 9. Unique Experiences in Switzerland

Visiting Chocolate and Cheese Factories

Visiting chocolate and cheese factories in Switzerland offers a unique and flavorful way to explore the country's rich culinary heritage. Switzerland is world-renowned for both its high-quality chocolate and its delicious cheese, making factory tours a must for food lovers. These visits not only provide insight into the production process but also offer the chance to indulge in tastings, learn about the craftsmanship behind the products, and bring home some of the finest treats Switzerland has to offer.

Switzerland's chocolate-making tradition dates back over a century, with some of the most famous brands known worldwide. A visit to a Swiss chocolate factory is a journey through the history and techniques that have made Swiss chocolate famous for its creamy texture and rich flavors. Many of the country's top chocolate producers, such as Maison Cailler in Broc and Lindt in Zurich, offer immersive factory tours. These tours typically begin with an overview of the history of chocolate, including its origins with the ancient civilizations of Central and South America and its introduction to Europe. You can learn how Swiss chocolatiers perfected their craft by combining local milk with the finest cocoa beans from around the world.

During a tour, visitors are often taken behind the scenes to see the chocolate-making process in action. From roasting cocoa beans to grinding and conching, each step is meticulously demonstrated. The transformation from raw ingredients to the finished product is fascinating, and you'll gain a deep appreciation for the skill involved in creating high-quality chocolate. Some factories also offer interactive experiences where visitors can try their hand at making their own chocolates, a fun and creative way to engage with Swiss traditions.

One of the highlights of visiting a chocolate factory is, of course, the tasting. Visitors are usually invited to sample a wide range of chocolates, from milk and dark varieties to those infused with exotic flavors or nuts. This is a great opportunity to taste freshly made chocolate, often considered some of the best in the world. Many factories also have gift shops where you can purchase an assortment of chocolates to take home, making for a perfect souvenir or gift.

Cheese is another iconic Swiss product, and factory visits offer a delicious exploration of how the country's most famous cheeses are made. Swiss cheese varieties such as Gruyère, Emmental, and Raclette are known for their distinctive flavors and textures, and they play a key role in traditional Swiss dishes like fondue and raclette. A visit to a cheese factory, like La Maison du Gruyère in the town of Gruyères, provides a glimpse into the artisanal techniques that have been passed down through generations of Swiss cheesemakers.

Cheese factory tours often begin with an introduction to the history of cheesemaking in Switzerland and the importance of cheese in Swiss culture. You'll learn about the different regions that produce specific types of cheese and how the climate, pastures, and altitude influence the taste and texture of each variety. The process of making Swiss cheese, particularly the aging and curing stages, is a critical part of what gives each cheese its unique character.

As you move through the factory, you'll see cheesemakers at work, transforming fresh milk into wheels of cheese using traditional methods. The use of copper vats, wooden molds, and careful aging in cellars all contribute to the creation of the perfect cheese. Depending on the time of year, you might even witness the making of Alpine cheeses, produced high in the mountains during the summer months when cows graze on fresh mountain pastures.

Tastings are a central part of the cheese factory experience. Visitors are invited to sample a variety of cheeses, often at different stages of maturity. This allows you to experience the progression of flavors, from mild and creamy young cheeses to strong, complex aged varieties. Some tours also include demonstrations on how to prepare Swiss specialties like fondue or raclette, giving you a taste of the traditional ways Swiss people enjoy their cheese.

Many cheese factories have on-site restaurants where you can savor local dishes made with the cheese produced right there. Whether it's a fondue meal or a plate of fresh cheese served with crusty bread and local wine, these meals offer a truly authentic Swiss dining experience. As with chocolate factories, cheese factories often have shops where you can purchase fresh cheese to take home, as well as other local products such as cured meats and jams.

For those interested in a deeper dive into both chocolate and cheese, Switzerland also offers combined tours or experiences that allow visitors to explore both crafts in a single day. These tours are a fantastic way to understand how Swiss culinary traditions have developed side by side, with cheese and chocolate playing an essential role in the country's identity.

Visiting chocolate and cheese factories in Switzerland is more than just a tasty excursion; it's a journey into the heart of the country's culinary heritage. The opportunity to witness the production process, sample fresh products, and learn about the traditions behind these iconic foods makes it a memorable experience for any traveler. Whether you're a food enthusiast or simply curious about Swiss culture, these factory tours provide a rich and rewarding way to connect with Switzerland's artisanal roots.

Hot Air Balloon Rides Over the Alps

Hot air balloon rides over the Alps offer one of the most breathtaking and unique ways to experience the majestic beauty of Switzerland's natural landscape. As the balloon slowly ascends, you are treated to an unparalleled view of the snow-capped peaks, verdant valleys, and crystal-clear lakes that define this iconic region. This serene and exhilarating experience allows you to glide over the rugged terrain and immerse yourself in the grandeur of the Alps in a way that few other modes of exploration can provide.

The journey begins early in the morning, typically at sunrise, when the winds are calm and the skies are clear. As the balloon rises gently into the sky, the panoramic views open up, revealing a sprawling tapestry of Alpine scenery. The stillness of the early morning air adds to the peaceful atmosphere, broken only by the occasional whoosh of the balloon's burner. From above, the jagged peaks of famous mountains like the Matterhorn, Mont Blanc, and the Eiger stand out against the horizon, providing a dramatic backdrop for your flight.

One of the highlights of hot air ballooning over the Alps is the sheer variety of landscapes you can witness. You'll float over serene alpine villages nestled in lush valleys, dense forests stretching across the slopes, and glacial rivers carving their way through the rugged terrain. The vibrant green pastures, dotted with grazing cows, contrast beautifully with the brilliant white snow that blankets the higher altitudes, creating a striking mosaic of color and texture. Depending on the weather and route, the flight may also take you over shimmering lakes such as Lake Geneva or Lake Thun, where the reflection of the mountains on the water creates an almost surreal visual experience.

The Alps are a year-round spectacle, and hot air ballooning is available in both summer and winter. In the warmer months, the meadows below come alive with wildflowers, and the snow retreats to the highest peaks, revealing rocky ridges and lush greenery. In winter, the landscape transforms into a winter wonderland, with everything blanketed in a layer of pristine snow. The contrast between the deep blue sky and the sparkling white snow below is particularly breathtaking in the colder months, offering a magical experience for those willing to brave the chill.

Ballooning over the Alps is not only about the views but also about the peaceful sense of detachment from the hustle and bustle of daily life. There is something inherently calming about drifting silently through the sky, free from the constraints of roads and trails. The gentle pace of the flight gives you time to appreciate the scale and beauty of the Alps, allowing for quiet reflection or simply the joy of being in the moment.

Many hot air balloon rides also include experienced pilots who share insights about the region's geography, history, and wildlife, enhancing the overall experience. They provide a narrative that helps you understand the significance of the landmarks below and may even point out hidden gems such as remote mountain huts or ancient glaciers that are only accessible by air. The pilots' deep knowledge of the local terrain adds a layer of appreciation for the sheer grandeur and complexity of the Alps.

Hot air balloon rides can also coincide with special events such as the International Hot Air Balloon Festival in Château-d'Oex. This event, held annually in January, attracts balloonists from around the world who gather to take part in mass ascensions, creating a sky filled with colorful balloons against the dramatic Alpine backdrop. Château-d'Oex is considered the ballooning capital of Switzerland, and the festival provides a truly spectacular sight, whether you are in the balloon or watching from the ground.

A hot air balloon ride over the Alps is suitable for a wide range of travelers, from couples seeking a romantic adventure to families looking for a memorable experience together. The slow and gentle nature of ballooning makes it accessible to almost anyone, with no particular physical requirements needed to enjoy the flight. Whether it's your first time in a hot air balloon or you're a seasoned enthusiast, flying over the Swiss Alps is an extraordinary way to connect with nature.

Balloon rides over the Alps provide a unique opportunity to experience the region from a different perspective. From the basket of a hot air balloon, the Alps take on a new dimension, revealing patterns and shapes that are impossible to see from the ground. The sense of wonder that comes from floating above such a rugged and dramatic landscape is something that stays with travelers long after they've landed.

At the end of the flight, as the balloon descends gracefully back to earth, there is often a tradition of toasting with a glass of champagne or sparkling wine, a fitting way to celebrate the incredible experience of having soared above one of the most beautiful mountain ranges in the world. The landing itself, gentle and smooth, brings you back to reality but leaves you with unforgettable memories of your journey above the Alps.

For those looking to experience the Alps in a truly unique and awe-inspiring way, a hot air balloon ride offers a once-in-a-lifetime adventure that perfectly captures the essence of Switzerland's natural beauty and tranquility.

Scenic Boat Rides on Lake Geneva and Lake Lucerne

Scenic boat rides on Lake Geneva and Lake Lucerne offer some of the most enchanting ways to explore

Switzerland's natural beauty. These lakes, surrounded by majestic mountains and picturesque towns, provide a tranquil escape and a unique perspective of the country's landscapes.

Lake Geneva, one of the largest freshwater lakes in Europe, lies on the border between Switzerland and France, with cities like Geneva, Montreux, and Lausanne offering easy access to the water. The lake's serene waters are cradled by the Alps, creating breathtaking scenery as the snow-capped peaks reflect in the clear blue waters. Boat cruises on Lake Geneva allow travelers to see iconic landmarks such as the Jet d'Eau in Geneva, a towering fountain that's one of the city's symbols. The lakeside towns along the way, like Montreux with its famous jazz festival, offer glimpses of Switzerland's cultural richness. One of the highlights of a cruise on Lake Geneva is the view of Chillon Castle, a medieval fortress perched on the lake's edge. This historic site, surrounded by water and mountains, seems almost frozen in time and provides a postcard-perfect moment for visitors. Cruises vary from short trips around the city of Geneva to longer excursions that take in the entire expanse of the lake, often stopping in charming villages along the way.

Lake Lucerne, nestled in the heart of Switzerland, is equally mesmerizing but offers a different kind of experience. The lake is smaller than Lake Geneva but is surrounded by towering mountains, including the famous Pilatus and Rigi peaks. This creates a dramatic landscape where the lake appears to be embraced by the rugged terrain, offering travelers the feeling of being completely immersed in nature. Boat rides on Lake Lucerne offer a unique combination of mountain and water views, with historic paddle steamers and modern motorboats ferrying passengers across the water. The city of Lucerne, with its medieval architecture and iconic Chapel Bridge, is the starting point for many cruises. As the boat glides away from the city, passengers are treated to sweeping views of the surrounding countryside, with traditional Swiss villages dotting the shores and the mountains rising in the background.

A particularly memorable aspect of cruising on Lake Lucerne is the ability to combine boat rides with other scenic activities. Many boat trips connect with cogwheel trains or cable cars, allowing visitors to ascend to nearby mountain peaks such as Pilatus or Rigi. This combination of boat and mountain excursions creates a quintessential Swiss experience, where travelers can enjoy the tranquility of the lake before being whisked to panoramic viewpoints high above. Another charming feature of Lake Lucerne is the opportunity to visit landmarks like the Swiss Museum of Transport or to stop at the car-free village of Weggis, where the beauty of the lake and mountains can be appreciated in peaceful seclusion.

Both lakes offer seasonal boat rides, with different types of cruises available depending on the time of year. In the summer, warm weather allows passengers to sit on open decks, soaking in the sun and the stunning alpine views. Autumn brings vibrant colors to the surrounding landscapes as the forests and vineyards along the shores turn golden, making fall boat rides especially scenic. In winter, while some services are reduced, special holiday-themed cruises are offered, creating a festive atmosphere as the snowy peaks and frosty lakeside villages complete the winter wonderland scene.

The boats themselves add a special charm to the experience. On Lake Geneva, many cruises take place aboard modern vessels, though traditional paddle steamers are also available, offering a more nostalgic journey through time. On Lake Lucerne, the historic paddle steamers are a major attraction in themselves, beautifully restored and offering a glimpse into Switzerland's maritime heritage. These steamers, with their gleaming brass fittings and wooden decks, transport travelers back to the early 20th century, adding a sense of elegance and romance to the journey.

On Lake Geneva, there are dinner cruises that combine fine dining with the breathtaking backdrop of the Alps and the lake's shimmering waters. On Lake Lucerne, similar themed cruises include brunch or sunset rides, where the colors of the setting sun reflect off the calm water, creating a magical end to the day. Themed events such as music nights or culinary voyages featuring Swiss specialties are also popular, offering a perfect blend of entertainment and scenic beauty.

Scenic boat rides on Lake Geneva and Lake Lucerne provide an unforgettable way to experience the natural wonders of Switzerland. The peaceful rhythm of the water, the majestic views of the surrounding mountains, and the charm of the lakeside towns create an idyllic atmosphere that captivates visitors. Whether you're seeking a leisurely sightseeing cruise or an adventurous journey that combines lakes and mountains, these boat rides offer a perfect mix of relaxation, exploration, and Swiss charm.

Exploring Underground Lakes and Ice Caves

Exploring underground lakes and ice caves in Switzerland offers an extraordinary glimpse into the hidden wonders beneath the surface of this beautiful country. These natural marvels, formed over millennia by geological processes, provide a rare opportunity to experience unique environments that contrast dramatically with the picturesque alpine landscapes above. Whether you are a nature lover, an adventurer, or simply looking for something different, these underground experiences are both awe-inspiring and educational.

One of the most famous underground lakes in Switzerland is the St. Léonard subterranean lake, located in the Valais region between Sion and Sierre. Known as Lac Souterrain de St-Léonard, it is the largest underground lake in Europe that can be explored by boat. This lake, hidden beneath the mountains, stretches over 300 meters in length and offers visitors a peaceful yet surreal boat ride through crystal-clear waters. Guided tours take you on a quiet journey through the caverns, where the dim lighting reflects off the water, creating a magical and serene atmosphere. The guides provide fascinating insights into the history and formation of the lake, explaining how it was carved by glaciers and how water seeps in from the surrounding rock formations. The constant cool temperature of the underground environment, combined with the echo of water dripping from the stone ceilings, adds to the mystical allure of the experience.

Switzerland is also home to some spectacular ice caves, where visitors can marvel at the intricate formations of ice and rock created by nature's slow and steady forces. The Rhône Glacier Ice Grotto is a particularly popular destination, located near the Furka Pass in the Swiss Alps. The glacier, which has been receding due to climate change, still offers an unforgettable glimpse into a world of ice and light. Each year, a tunnel is carved into the glacier, allowing visitors to walk through an ethereal blue ice grotto. The experience of walking inside a glacier is surreal, as the ice walls glow with a soft blue hue, making it feel as though you have stepped into another world. The ice formations change slightly each year, so no two visits are exactly the same. The Rhône Glacier is also one of the few remaining glaciers in the world that allows this kind of access, providing a rare opportunity to experience the fragile beauty of these ancient ice masses up close.

Another fascinating ice cave can be found at the Titlis Glacier, near the famous Mount Titlis in central Switzerland. The Ice Cave at Titlis is accessible via a revolving cable car, which itself offers stunning panoramic views of the surrounding mountains. Once inside the cave, visitors can wander through a labyrinth of ice tunnels that extend deep beneath the glacier. The cave maintains a constant temperature below freezing, and the icy walls are illuminated with soft lights, highlighting the natural beauty of the frozen formations. The Ice Cave at Titlis is a particularly family-friendly destination, offering an educational and visually captivating experience for all ages.

The Trummelbach Falls, though not a lake or ice cave, are another underground marvel worth exploring. Located in the Lauterbrunnen Valley, the Trummelbach Falls are a series of glacial waterfalls hidden inside a mountain. These falls are fed by the melting glaciers of the Eiger, Mönch, and Jungfrau, and their powerful torrents of water carve their way through the rock, creating a dramatic spectacle. A series of tunnels, walkways, and lifts allow visitors to explore the various levels of the falls, where you can feel the force of the water as it thunders down through the narrow gorges. The experience is both exhilarating and humbling, as the raw power of nature is on full display.

Exploring these underground lakes and ice caves provides a unique perspective on the natural forces that have shaped Switzerland's landscapes. While the alpine peaks and rolling green valleys are well-known and frequently photographed, the subterranean and glacial environments are often overlooked, making them all the more special for those who seek them out. These experiences not only offer a sense of adventure but also remind visitors of the fragility of these ecosystems. Many of the glaciers, for example, are receding due to global warming, and their ice caves may not be accessible forever.

Visiting these underground and ice-filled environments also requires some preparation. Temperatures inside ice caves and subterranean lakes tend to be quite low, even during the summer months, so it's important to dress warmly and wear appropriate footwear. Guided tours are often the best way to explore these sites, as the guides provide valuable safety information and insights into the geological history of the region. Most of these sites are accessible to visitors of all ages and fitness levels, though some, like the ice caves, may involve walking on uneven or slippery surfaces.

Exploring Switzerland's underground lakes and ice caves is a breathtaking experience that takes you into the heart of nature's hidden realms. Whether you're gliding across the tranquil waters of an underground lake or wandering through the luminous corridors of a glacier, these unique adventures offer a rare opportunity to connect with the earth's natural beauty in a way that few other experiences can. It's a journey into the depths of Switzerland that leaves a lasting impression, both for its beauty and for the sense of wonder it inspires.

Chapter 10. Practical Information

Language and Communication

Switzerland is a linguistically diverse country with four official languages: German, French, Italian, and Romansh. This multilingualism reflects the nation's geographic and cultural proximity to its neighbors—Germany, France, Italy, and Austria—and its historical roots as a federation of different regions. The use of multiple languages in Switzerland is one of the country's defining characteristics, and understanding the linguistic landscape can greatly enhance your travel experience.

The most widely spoken language in Switzerland is Swiss German, or "Schweizerdeutsch," which is used by about 60 to 65 percent of the population. However, Swiss German is not a single language but rather a group of Alemannic dialects spoken across different regions. The variation in dialects can be quite pronounced, even within small geographic areas, and they are distinct from the standard German (Hochdeutsch) taught in schools and used in formal writing, news broadcasts, and official documents. Most Swiss Germans switch to standard German when necessary, especially in professional settings or when communicating with non-Swiss speakers of German. For travelers, this means that if you know standard German, you will still be able to communicate effectively in the German-speaking parts of Switzerland, especially in cities like Zurich, Basel, and Bern. However, you may find the Swiss dialects challenging to understand in casual conversation.

In the western part of Switzerland, French is the dominant language, spoken by about 20 to 25 percent of the population. This region, known as Romandy, includes cities such as Geneva, Lausanne, and Neuchâtel. The French spoken in Switzerland is very similar to that spoken in France, with only minor differences in vocabulary and pronunciation. Travelers who speak French will have no difficulty communicating in this part of the country. The French-speaking Swiss tend to be comfortable switching to other languages, such as English, when necessary, particularly in cosmopolitan cities like Geneva, which hosts numerous international organizations and expatriates.

In the southern canton of Ticino and parts of the southern valleys, Italian is the primary language, spoken by roughly 8 percent of the population. The Italian spoken in Switzerland is standard Italian, though there are regional dialects and influences from neighboring Italy. Cities like Lugano and Locarno are part of the Italian-speaking region, and travelers familiar with Italian will find it easy to communicate here. The region's proximity to Italy also means that many aspects of Italian culture, including cuisine and architecture, are prominently reflected in the area.

Romansh, the fourth official language of Switzerland, is spoken by a much smaller percentage of the population—less than 1 percent—and is concentrated mainly in the canton of Graubünden in the eastern part of the country. Romansh is a Romance language with several distinct dialects, some of which have been standardized into a form known as Rumantsch Grischun. Although Romansh is recognized as an official language, its usage has been declining, and it is now primarily used in rural areas. Travelers are unlikely to encounter Romansh outside of these regions, and most Romansh speakers are bilingual, also fluent in Swiss German or another national language.

English plays an increasingly important role in Switzerland, particularly in business, tourism, and higher education. Many Swiss people, especially younger generations and those working in urban areas or international sectors, speak English fluently. This makes it relatively easy for English-speaking travelers to get around the country, especially in cities like Zurich, Geneva, and Lucerne, where English signage and information are common. English is often used as a neutral language in multilingual settings, particularly in corporate environments where people from different linguistic regions come together. In tourist areas, such as ski resorts or major cultural attractions, English is widely spoken by staff and service providers.

One unique aspect of communication in Switzerland is the high degree of linguistic tolerance and flexibility among the Swiss people. Due to the multilingual nature of the country, it is common for Swiss citizens to be proficient in more than one language. Many Swiss grow up learning at least two national languages in school, in addition to English, which is typically introduced in the curriculum at an early age. This linguistic adaptability means that even if you find yourself in a region where your preferred language is not spoken, there is a good chance you will be able to communicate effectively.

However, it's important to note that while Swiss people are accommodating, they also appreciate when visitors make an effort to use the local language, even if it's just a few basic phrases. Greeting someone in their native language, such as saying "Grüezi" in German-speaking areas, "Bonjour" in French-speaking regions, or "Buongiorno" in Italian-speaking parts, is always appreciated and can help create a positive interaction. This small gesture can go a long way in showing respect for the local culture.

Communication is usually conducted in the language of the particular region. Government documents, public signage, and legal matters are typically handled in the local language. For example, in Zurich, official notices and documents are written in German, while in Geneva, they would be in French. This linguistic division is reflected in the media as well. Newspapers, television channels, and radio stations operate primarily in the local language of the region, though some national outlets offer multilingual content. Major cities often have a range of media options, including international newspapers and English-language news channels.

Switzerland's linguistic diversity is a testament to its multicultural identity and offers travelers the opportunity to experience several European languages and cultures within one country. Whether you are wandering through the French-speaking streets of Geneva, exploring the Italian charm of Lugano, or immersing yourself in the German dialects of Zurich, language is an essential part of the Swiss experience. Understanding and embracing this diversity can enrich your journey and deepen your appreciation of the country's unique cultural fabric.

Currency and Tipping Etiquette

Switzerland's official currency is the Swiss Franc, abbreviated as CHF, and commonly denoted by the symbol Fr or SFr. While Switzerland is located in the heart of Europe and surrounded by countries that use the Euro, it has maintained its own currency. The Swiss Franc is divided into 100 smaller units called centimes in French, Rappen in German, or centesimi in Italian, depending on the region. Swiss Franc notes are issued in denominations of 10, 20, 50, 100, 200, and 1000 francs, while coins are available in denominations of 5, 10, 20, and 50 centimes, as well as 1, 2, and 5 francs.

Despite Switzerland not using the Euro, many businesses, especially in major tourist areas, do accept euros. However, it's important to note that the exchange rate might not be favorable, and any change will likely be given in Swiss Francs. For this reason, it is generally more cost-effective to use Swiss Francs for transactions. Credit and debit cards are widely accepted throughout Switzerland, and ATMs are readily available in cities and towns, allowing travelers to withdraw Swiss Francs easily. It is advisable to carry some cash, particularly in rural areas or for small purchases, as not every establishment may accept cards.

When it comes to tipping etiquette in Switzerland, it is quite different from many other countries. In most cases, service charges are included in the price of goods and services, whether at restaurants, hotels, or for other services. This means that tipping is not strictly required or expected. However, it is common practice to round up the bill slightly as a gesture of appreciation for good service. For instance, if your restaurant bill comes to 47 francs, you might round it up to 50 francs or leave a small amount as a tip. The same applies when taking a taxi or receiving services at a café or bar.

In restaurants, it is perfectly acceptable to round up to the nearest whole number, as Swiss servers are paid fair wages, and gratuity is already factored into the bill. If you feel that the service was particularly good, you can certainly leave an additional tip, though it is typically modest, usually not exceeding 5-10 percent of the total bill. When paying by card, it's common to indicate the total amount, including the tip, when the card reader prompts you, or you can leave cash on the table.

In more casual settings, such as cafés, bars, or for takeaway orders, rounding up the bill is sufficient. For instance, if you buy a coffee for 4.50 francs, you could leave 5 francs. This small gesture is appreciated but not obligatory.

Tipping for other services, such as hotel staff, varies. For porters, it is customary to give around one or two francs per bag, while housekeeping staff might receive a small tip of one or two francs per day if you feel the service was exceptional. If you use the services of a concierge for special arrangements or bookings, tipping a few francs as a thank you is a nice gesture, though again, not mandatory.

In taxis, tipping is not a strict requirement, but rounding up the fare to the nearest franc is common practice. If the driver provides extra help, such as assisting with luggage or offering useful travel tips, you might tip a few extra francs to show your appreciation. However, Swiss taxi drivers, like restaurant staff, do not expect large tips, as service charges are factored into the fare.

For other services, such as hairdressers, spa treatments, or tour guides, tipping is appreciated but not essential. A small tip of a few francs for exceptional service is considered polite, but most Swiss service providers do not rely on tips for their income, given that wages are generally higher compared to many other countries.

It is also worth noting that when tipping, it is not common to leave the money on the table or hand it directly to the person in a formal manner. Instead, tipping is done discreetly, often by rounding up the total when paying, and the process is very low-key. There is no pressure to tip, and it is generally left to your discretion based on the level of service you received.

Switzerland's tipping culture is relatively relaxed compared to other countries, with no obligation to tip beyond what is included in the bill. The Swiss value quality service, but this is already reflected in their pricing. Tipping, while appreciated, is usually modest and should be viewed as a small gesture of gratitude rather than a requirement. Familiarizing yourself with these practices will help you navigate everyday transactions and ensure that you contribute to Swiss customs respectfully.

Visa Requirements and Travel Insurance

When planning a trip to Switzerland, understanding visa requirements and travel insurance is crucial for ensuring a smooth and enjoyable experience. Switzerland, being part of the Schengen Area, has specific visa policies that vary depending on your nationality and the length of your stay.

For citizens of many countries, including the United States, Canada, Australia, and New Zealand, a visa is not required for short stays of up to 90 days within a 180-day period for tourism or business purposes. Travelers can enter Switzerland with just a valid passport, provided that it is valid for at least three months beyond the intended departure date from the Schengen Area. Additionally, the passport should have been issued within the last ten years. However, it is essential to check specific entry requirements based on your nationality, as regulations may change and vary.

For those who plan to stay in Switzerland for longer than 90 days or who intend to work or study, a visa is required. The type of visa you will need depends on your purpose of stay. Long-stay visas include student visas, work permits, and family reunification visas, each with its own application process. It is advisable to apply for a visa at the Swiss consulate or embassy in your home country well in advance of your travel dates. The application process may involve submitting documents such as proof of accommodation, financial means, health insurance, and a valid travel itinerary.

Travelers should also be aware of the European Travel Information and Authorization System (ETIAS), which is expected to come into effect soon. Under this new system, citizens from visa-exempt countries will need to obtain an electronic travel authorization before entering the Schengen Area, including Switzerland. This authorization will be valid for multiple entries and will streamline the entry process for tourists and business travelers alike.

Securing travel insurance is a vital step in preparing for your trip. While Switzerland is known for its high standard of healthcare, medical costs can be extremely expensive for travelers without insurance. Therefore, having travel insurance that covers medical expenses, trip cancellations, and lost belongings can provide peace of mind during your travels.

Travel insurance policies can vary widely, so it's important to carefully review the coverage options available. Basic policies often cover emergency medical expenses, hospitalization, and repatriation in the event of severe illness or injury. However, comprehensive plans may also include coverage for trip cancellation or interruption, lost luggage, travel delays, and even personal liability. When selecting a policy, consider your specific travel needs, such as pre-existing medical conditions, adventure activities planned during your stay, and any additional coverage you may require.

Many insurance providers offer policies tailored specifically for international travelers. It is wise to compare different plans and read reviews to choose a reputable provider. Additionally, some credit card companies offer travel insurance as a perk for cardholders, so check the benefits associated with your card before purchasing a separate policy.

When obtaining travel insurance, it is crucial to keep documentation handy. This includes a copy of your insurance policy, emergency contact information, and any necessary medical documentation, particularly if you have pre-existing conditions. Should an emergency arise, having this information readily available will facilitate quicker access to care and support.

Understanding the visa requirements and securing travel insurance are essential components of planning a successful trip to Switzerland. By being aware of the regulations regarding entry and ensuring you have adequate coverage, you can enjoy your journey with confidence, knowing you are prepared for any unexpected circumstances. Whether you are marveling at the stunning landscapes, savoring Swiss chocolate, or exploring the rich cultural heritage, taking these steps will help ensure a smooth and memorable experience in Switzerland.

Safety Tips and Emergency Contacts

First and foremost, always stay aware of your surroundings. While Switzerland is known for its safety, petty crime such as pickpocketing can occur in crowded tourist areas and public transportation. Keep your belongings secure, and consider using a money belt or a secure bag. Avoid displaying valuable items such as expensive cameras or jewelry, which can attract unwanted attention. When using public transportation, be vigilant, especially during busy hours, and keep your bags close to you.

Health and wellness are also important aspects of travel safety. Before embarking on your journey, check if you have adequate travel insurance that covers medical emergencies, trip cancellations, and lost belongings. Ensure your vaccinations are up to date, and carry any necessary medications in their original packaging, along with a copy of your prescriptions. If you have specific health concerns, research local medical facilities and pharmacies in the areas you plan to visit. Swiss cities generally have excellent healthcare services, but it's advisable to be aware of your options in case of illness or injury.

When it comes to outdoor activities, Switzerland's breathtaking landscapes invite adventure, but they also require caution. Whether you're hiking, skiing, or engaging in other outdoor pursuits, always check the weather conditions before heading out. Sudden weather changes can occur in the mountains, and being caught unprepared can be dangerous. Dress in layers to accommodate fluctuating temperatures and ensure you have proper equipment for your activities, including sturdy footwear and navigation tools.

For hiking, stick to well-marked trails and consider investing in a good map or a reliable GPS device. Inform someone about your plans and estimated return time, especially if you are hiking alone or in remote areas. Pay attention to trail signs and always heed warnings about difficult or dangerous paths. If you're skiing, familiarize yourself with the slopes and be aware of your skill level; choose runs that match your experience to avoid accidents.

In case of emergencies, knowing the local emergency contacts is crucial. The general emergency number in Switzerland is 112, which you can call for police, fire, and medical emergencies. For more specific needs, you can reach the police at 117, fire services at 118, and ambulance services at 144. It is advisable to keep a list of important numbers readily accessible, including your accommodation's contact information, local emergency services, and your country's embassy or consulate. The embassy can assist you with various issues, including lost passports, legal matters, or health emergencies.

Familiarize yourself with local laws and regulations. Each canton in Switzerland may have its own rules, particularly concerning outdoor activities, alcohol consumption, and driving. Respect these regulations to avoid fines or other legal issues. For example, in some areas, outdoor fires are prohibited, and noise regulations may be stricter in residential neighborhoods.

Understanding these nuances will help you have a more respectful and enjoyable visit.

Traveling during the winter months can present additional safety considerations, particularly regarding snow and ice. If you plan to drive, ensure your vehicle is equipped with winter tires, and be prepared for changing road conditions. Always check road conditions before setting out, and consider using public transportation, which is often more reliable during snowy weather. If you find yourself in a situation where you cannot drive safely, do not hesitate to seek help or use alternative transportation options.

In urban areas, it's important to stay aware of traffic patterns, particularly when crossing streets. Swiss cities are pedestrian-friendly, but be cautious at crosswalks and always follow traffic signals. If you are cycling, make sure to adhere to local cycling laws, wear a helmet, and use designated bike lanes whenever possible.

When it comes to personal safety, trust your instincts. If a situation feels uncomfortable or unsafe, remove yourself from it as soon as possible. It's also wise to keep your accommodation information and important documents, such as your passport and travel insurance details, in a secure location. Consider making photocopies of essential documents and storing them separately in case of loss or theft.

Lastly, always maintain a positive attitude and engage with the local culture. Learning a few phrases in the local language can go a long way in fostering goodwill and connection with Swiss residents. Locals are generally friendly and willing to help, so don't hesitate to ask for assistance if you need directions or recommendations.

While Switzerland is a safe travel destination, being prepared and aware of safety tips can significantly enhance your experience. By staying vigilant, knowing emergency contacts, and respecting local regulations, you can enjoy the beauty and culture of Switzerland with peace of mind. The country's stunning landscapes, rich history, and welcoming atmosphere make it a remarkable place to explore, and being well-prepared will ensure your travels are as smooth and enjoyable as possible.

Chapter 11. Suggested Itineraries

3-Day Switzerland Highlights

A three-day journey through Switzerland offers a tantalizing glimpse of the country's diverse landscapes, vibrant cities, and rich cultural heritage. While it's impossible to see everything in such a short time, this itinerary provides a balanced mix of stunning natural beauty and urban exploration, ensuring an unforgettable experience.

Starting in Zurich, Switzerland's largest city, the journey begins with a morning stroll along Lake Zurich. The lake, surrounded by picturesque mountains, offers a serene atmosphere ideal for a leisurely walk. Visitors can explore the charming streets of the Old Town, where historic buildings and narrow alleys invite discovery. Highlights include the iconic Grossmünster church with its twin towers, the beautiful Fraumünster with its famous Chagall stained glass windows, and the vibrant Lindenhof hill, which provides panoramic views of the city. A visit to the Swiss National Museum can provide insight into Switzerland's cultural history, showcasing artifacts from different eras.

After immersing yourself in the urban charm of Zurich, the journey continues to Lucerne, a short train ride away. The scenic train ride itself is a highlight, with breathtaking views of rolling hills and the Alps. In

Lucerne, visitors are greeted by a stunning lakeside setting and a backdrop of towering mountains. The city is famous for its well-preserved medieval architecture, including the Chapel Bridge, adorned with flowers and artwork depicting historical events. A leisurely walk along the promenade of Lake Lucerne offers spectacular views of the surrounding peaks, including Mount Pilatus and Mount Rigi.

An essential activity in Lucerne is taking a boat trip on Lake Lucerne, where travelers can enjoy the serene beauty of the water and mountains from the comfort of a ferry. Options include a short cruise or a longer journey to nearby villages such as Weggis or Vitznau, where hiking trails lead to stunning viewpoints. Another highlight is the Lion Monument, a poignant sculpture commemorating Swiss Guards who died during the French Revolution, which embodies Switzerland's commitment to honor its history.

On the second day, the adventure continues with a visit to Interlaken, nestled between Lake Thun and Lake Brienz. The journey from Lucerne to Interlaken takes travelers through picturesque landscapes, offering views of valleys and mountains. Interlaken serves as a gateway to the Jungfrau region, known for its stunning alpine scenery. Here, visitors can take a cogwheel train to Jungfraujoch, the "Top of Europe," where they can explore the Aletsch Glacier, the largest glacier in the Alps. At Jungfraujoch, the views from the observation deck are breathtaking, with panoramic vistas of snow-capped peaks and deep valleys.

In the afternoon, travelers can explore Interlaken itself, where they can stroll through the charming streets, visit local shops, and sample Swiss delicacies. For adventure seekers, the region offers a plethora of outdoor activities, including hiking, paragliding, and even summer tobogganing. The vibrant atmosphere of Interlaken, with its stunning scenery and range of activities, ensures an exciting day for all.

On the final day, the itinerary shifts to Geneva, where a blend of history, culture, and natural beauty awaits. A morning train from Interlaken to Geneva offers a relaxing transition to the city. Upon arrival, visitors can explore the iconic Jet d'Eau, the large water fountain in Lake Geneva that has become a symbol of the city. A walk along the lakeshore reveals beautiful parks and gardens, perfect for a leisurely stroll.

The Old Town of Geneva, with its narrow cobblestone streets, is a treasure trove of historical sites. The St. Pierre Cathedral, with its impressive tower offering panoramic views of the city, is a must-visit. Nearby, the Place du Bourg-de-Four is a charming square filled with cafes and shops, ideal for enjoying a coffee while soaking in the local atmosphere.

For those interested in international affairs, a visit to the United Nations Office at Geneva provides insight into the city's role as a diplomatic hub. Guided tours offer a look at the assembly halls and the famous "Broken Chair" sculpture, a powerful symbol of the fight against landmines.

In the afternoon, exploring the International Red Cross and Red Crescent Museum can provide a profound understanding of humanitarian efforts. The museum's engaging exhibitions and interactive displays make for an informative and moving experience.

As the day draws to a close, visitors can unwind in the Parc des Bastions, home to the Reformation Wall, which commemorates the leaders of the Protestant Reformation. This peaceful park is the perfect spot to reflect on the journey through Switzerland while enjoying the beauty of the surrounding gardens.

A three-day highlight tour of Switzerland offers a rich tapestry of experiences, from the urban charm of Zurich to the alpine beauty of Interlaken and the cultural depth of Geneva. Each destination showcases the diverse offerings of this enchanting country, ensuring that travelers leave with lasting memories and a deep appreciation for Switzerland's natural and cultural heritage.

7-Day Tour of the Swiss Alps

A 7-day tour of the Swiss Alps is an exhilarating journey through some of the most breathtaking landscapes in the world. From majestic mountains to picturesque villages, this itinerary showcases the natural beauty, rich culture, and exhilarating outdoor activities that define this iconic region. Each day of the tour is packed with adventures, stunning sights, and opportunities to immerse yourself in the alpine lifestyle.

The journey begins in Zurich, Switzerland's largest city and a gateway to the Alps. After arriving in Zurich, take some time to explore the vibrant city. Stroll along the beautiful Lake Zurich promenade, visit the historic Old Town with its charming cobblestone streets, and discover the many museums and galleries, such as the Swiss National Museum. Zurich is also known for its culinary scene, so be sure to enjoy a traditional Swiss meal at a local restaurant before embarking on your alpine adventure.

On the second day, set out for Lucerne, a charming city nestled between the mountains and Lake Lucerne. The drive or train ride from Zurich to Lucerne takes about an hour and offers stunning views of the surrounding landscape. Once in Lucerne, explore the famous Chapel Bridge, visit the impressive Lion Monument, and take a leisurely walk along the lake. In the afternoon, take a boat ride on Lake Lucerne, surrounded by towering mountains and quaint villages. As the day winds down, consider taking a sunset cruise to fully appreciate the beauty of the lake and its surroundings.

The next day, embark on a day trip to Mount Pilatus or Mount Rigi, both easily accessible from Lucerne. Mount Pilatus offers breathtaking panoramic views of the Swiss Alps and the surrounding lakes. You can reach the summit via the world's steepest cogwheel railway or a scenic gondola ride. Once at the top, enjoy hiking trails that range from easy walks to more challenging routes. Alternatively, if you choose Mount Rigi, known as the "Queen of the Mountains," you can hike or take a cable car to the summit for equally stunning views. Both mountains offer numerous opportunities for outdoor activities and photo opportunities.

On the fourth day, travel to Interlaken, a popular destination for adventure seekers located between Lake Thun and Lake Brienz. The journey from Lucerne to Interlaken takes approximately two hours by train. Upon arrival, explore the charming town and take in the stunning views of the Eiger, Mönch, and Jungfrau mountains. Interlaken is renowned for its outdoor activities, so consider trying paragliding or a thrilling boat ride on one of the lakes. In the evening, relax in a local café or restaurant, enjoying the Swiss cuisine and the lively atmosphere of the town.

The fifth day is dedicated to exploring the Jungfrau region, one of the most spectacular areas in the Swiss Alps. Take the cogwheel train from Interlaken to Jungfraujoch, known as the "Top of Europe." The train ride takes you through breathtaking landscapes, past stunning waterfalls, and charming alpine villages. Once you reach Jungfraujoch, you'll be greeted by views of the Aletsch Glacier, the longest glacier in the Alps. Explore the observation deck, visit the Ice Palace, and take in the majestic vistas. Spend some time walking around and soaking up the atmosphere before descending back to Interlaken in the late afternoon.

On the sixth day, travel to Zermatt, home of the iconic Matterhorn. The journey takes about three hours by train, with the last leg requiring a scenic ride on the Gornergrat Railway, which offers stunning views of the Matterhorn. Once in Zermatt, take a leisurely stroll through the car-free village, enjoying its charming architecture and local shops. For a breathtaking view of the Matterhorn, take the Gornergrat Railway to the summit, where you can marvel at the surrounding peaks and enjoy a meal at the mountaintop restaurant. Zermatt is also an excellent base for hiking and skiing, depending on the season.

On the final day of your tour, return to Zurich for your departure or to extend your stay in Switzerland. If time permits, consider stopping in the charming town of Bern, the capital of Switzerland, along the way. Bern's UNESCO World Heritage-listed Old Town is a delightful place to explore, with its medieval architecture, arcades, and the iconic Zytglogge clock tower. Stroll along the Aare River, visit the Federal Palace, and take in the vibrant atmosphere before concluding your Swiss Alps adventure.

A 7-day tour of the Swiss Alps is a captivating experience that blends breathtaking scenery with thrilling outdoor activities and rich cultural encounters. Each day offers a unique glimpse into the diverse landscapes and charming towns that define this stunning region. From the urban elegance of Zurich to the serene beauty of alpine lakes and the majesty of towering peaks, this itinerary is sure to leave a lasting impression and inspire a deep appreciation for the wonders of the Swiss Alps.

Two Weeks in Switzerland: A Comprehensive Tour

A two-week tour of Switzerland offers an incredible opportunity to explore the diverse landscapes, vibrant cities, and rich cultural heritage of this stunning country. From the snow-capped peaks of the Alps to the charming lakeside towns, this itinerary captures the essence of Switzerland while providing a balance of adventure, relaxation, and cultural immersion.

The journey often begins in Zurich, Switzerland's largest city and a major international gateway. Known for its vibrant arts scene and stunning lake views, Zurich is the perfect place to start your Swiss adventure. Spend your first day exploring the charming Old Town, where cobblestone streets wind between historic buildings, boutiques, and cafes. Visit the renowned Kunsthaus, which houses an impressive collection of Swiss and international art, and take a stroll along the banks of Lake Zurich. A boat ride on the lake offers beautiful views of the surrounding mountains and the city skyline. Don't miss the opportunity to sample traditional Swiss cuisine at one of the many restaurants, perhaps indulging in fondue or raclette, which are quintessential Swiss dishes.

After soaking in Zurich, head to Lucerne, a picturesque city nestled between Lake Lucerne and the surrounding mountains. The journey by train offers breathtaking views of the countryside, making the trip part of the experience. In Lucerne, visit the iconic Chapel Bridge and the Water Tower, two of the city's most famous landmarks. Explore the Swiss Museum of Transport, which showcases the history of Swiss transportation through interactive exhibits. For a memorable adventure, take a day trip to Mount Pilatus or Mount Rigi, where you can hike or take a cogwheel train to the summits for panoramic views of the Swiss Alps and the shimmering lake below.

From Lucerne, continue your journey to Interlaken, a hub for outdoor enthusiasts located between Lake Thun and Lake Brienz. Interlaken serves as a base for numerous adventure activities, including hiking, paragliding, and boat trips. Spend a day exploring the surrounding area, perhaps taking a scenic train ride to the Jungfrau region. Visit Jungfraujoch, known as the "Top of Europe," where you can marvel at the Aletsch Glacier and enjoy breathtaking views of the Bernese Alps. For those seeking a more leisurely experience, a boat ride on Lake Thun allows you to relax while soaking in the stunning alpine scenery.

After experiencing the thrill of Interlaken, head to the charming village of Lauterbrunnen, known for its stunning waterfalls and dramatic cliffs. Take a short hike to the Trummelbach Falls, a series of impressive waterfalls hidden inside a mountain, and visit the nearby Staubbach Falls, which cascades down from a height of 300 meters. Lauterbrunnen serves as a gateway to the Schilthorn and Piz Gloria, offering a unique opportunity to ride the cable car to the summit for stunning views and a chance to dine in the revolving restaurant.

Next on the itinerary is the enchanting town of Zermatt, home to the iconic Matterhorn. The journey to Zermatt requires a scenic train ride, with views of the alpine landscapes along the way. Once in Zermatt, explore the charming car-free village, where wooden chalets and boutique shops line the streets. Take the Gornergrat railway to the summit for a breathtaking panoramic view of the Matterhorn and the surrounding peaks. Zermatt also offers fantastic hiking opportunities, with trails suitable for various skill levels. In winter, Zermatt is a haven for skiing and snowboarding enthusiasts.

From Zermatt, make your way to the culturally rich city of Bern, the capital of Switzerland. The historic old town, a UNESCO World Heritage site, is characterized by medieval architecture, cobbled streets, and the famous Zytglogge clock tower. Take time to explore the Bear Park, visit the Federal Palace, and stroll along the Aare River. Bern's vibrant atmosphere and numerous cafes make it an excellent place to relax and enjoy local pastries, such as the famous Bernese meringue.

Following Bern, continue to Geneva, a cosmopolitan city located on the shores of Lake Geneva. Known for its international organizations, including the United Nations, Geneva is a melting pot of cultures and languages. Explore the beautiful Parc des Bastions, home to the Reformation Wall, and visit the Jet d'Eau, the iconic fountain that shoots water high into the air. Take a stroll along the lake promenade, where you can enjoy picturesque views of the Alps and the surrounding vineyards. Geneva is also known for its diverse culinary scene, with numerous restaurants offering global cuisine and local specialties.

Next, head to Lausanne, located just a short train ride from Geneva. This vibrant city is home to the Olympic Museum, which celebrates the history of the Olympic Games through interactive exhibits and beautiful gardens. Lausanne's hilly landscape offers stunning views of Lake Geneva and the Alps, making it a picturesque destination. Spend time exploring the Old Town, with its charming streets, boutiques, and cafes.

After Lausanne, consider a visit to the Lavaux vineyards, a UNESCO World Heritage site known for its terraced vineyards overlooking Lake Geneva. Enjoy a wine tasting tour at one of the local wineries and take in the breathtaking views of the lake and mountains. The region is also ideal for leisurely hikes along the vineyards, allowing you to appreciate the stunning landscape.

Finally, conclude your two-week adventure in Switzerland with a visit to Montreux, a glamorous town famous for its annual jazz festival and beautiful lakeside promenade. Explore the Chillon Castle, perched on the shores of Lake Geneva, and stroll along the flower-lined path that connects Montreux to Villeneuve. The region is also known for its stunning gardens and parks, offering a tranquil atmosphere to relax and reflect on your Swiss journey.

Throughout this two-week tour, travelers will experience the unparalleled beauty of Switzerland, from its vibrant cities to its breathtaking natural landscapes. The combination of adventure, culture, and stunning scenery makes Switzerland a destination that leaves a lasting impression, ensuring that visitors will cherish their memories of this remarkable country for years to come.

Chapter 12.. Packing Tips for Switzerland

Seasonal Clothing Guide

Switzerland's diverse climate and varying altitudes mean that seasonal clothing choices are essential for enjoying all the country has to offer throughout the year. Whether you are exploring the vibrant cities, hiking in the mountains, or skiing on the slopes, being adequately prepared with the right clothing can significantly enhance your experience.

During the winter months, Switzerland transforms into a picturesque wonderland, especially in the alpine regions. Warmth and insulation are critical during this time, as temperatures can plunge well below freezing. Layering is a smart strategy, allowing you to adjust your clothing based on the temperature and activity level. Start with a moisture-wicking base layer, such as thermal underwear made from synthetic fabrics or merino wool. This layer will help keep you dry and warm by drawing sweat away from your skin.

For your mid-layer, consider wearing a fleece or wool sweater, which provides insulation while remaining breathable. An insulated jacket, preferably waterproof or windproof, is essential for the outer layer. Look for options with features such as adjustable hoods, cuffs, and ventilation zippers to enhance comfort while engaging in outdoor activities. Accessories play a crucial role in winter as well; a warm hat, scarf, and gloves are necessary to protect your extremities from the cold. Don't forget thermal socks and waterproof boots designed for winter conditions, especially if you plan on hiking or spending time in snow-covered areas.

Spring in Switzerland marks a transition period, with temperatures gradually rising and days becoming longer. However, the weather can still be quite unpredictable, so dressing in layers remains key. A light, waterproof jacket is advisable, as spring showers can be frequent. Underneath, a long-sleeve shirt or light sweater provides comfort during cooler mornings and evenings. As temperatures increase throughout the day, you can easily remove layers. Comfortable trousers or jeans are suitable for casual outings, but consider bringing lighter materials for warmer days. Footwear should be versatile; waterproof shoes or hiking boots are excellent choices, especially if you plan to explore the beautiful blooming landscapes or venture into the mountains.

As summer arrives, Switzerland enjoys warm and sunny days, particularly in the lowlands and cities. Lightweight and breathable fabrics become essential for staying cool and comfortable. Opt for short-sleeve shirts or blouses made of cotton or linen, which are breathable and wick away moisture. Shorts, skirts, or lightweight trousers will keep you comfortable during the heat. A wide-brimmed hat and sunglasses are also necessary to protect yourself from the sun while exploring outdoor attractions.

In mountainous areas, temperatures can still be cool, even in summer, particularly at higher elevations. A light jacket or a fleece can be useful for cooler evenings or when hiking at higher altitudes. Waterproof shoes are advisable for hiking, as trails can be rocky and uneven, and sudden rain showers can occur. Swimwear is a great addition if you plan to visit lakes or pools, as many Swiss lakes offer pristine swimming opportunities during the summer months.

As autumn approaches, the weather begins to cool again, and the stunning fall foliage transforms the landscape. Layering remains important as temperatures fluctuate. A warm sweater or fleece will be essential for layering under a waterproof jacket during occasional rain showers. Long pants or jeans are suitable for most outings, and comfortable, sturdy shoes or boots are recommended for walking through scenic trails or exploring the cities. As the days shorten, bringing a scarf and gloves can help keep you warm during chillier evenings.

Accessories are essential for adapting to Switzerland's varied climate throughout the seasons. A good-quality backpack is helpful for day trips, allowing you to carry extra layers, water, and snacks. An umbrella or a packable rain jacket can be lifesavers when encountering unexpected weather, especially in the spring and fall.

A seasonal clothing guide for Switzerland emphasizes the importance of layers, breathability, and comfort in accommodating the country's diverse climate. By choosing the right clothing and accessories for each season, travelers can fully enjoy all that Switzerland has to offer, from stunning mountain hikes to vibrant city explorations, while remaining comfortable and prepared for whatever the weather may bring.

Travel Gear for Outdoor Activities

When embarking on outdoor adventures in Switzerland, having the right travel gear is essential for ensuring comfort, safety, and enjoyment. The diverse landscapes of the country, from the rugged Alps to serene lakes, offer countless opportunities for hiking, skiing, climbing, and exploring. Being well-equipped can significantly enhance your experience and help you make the most of your time in the great outdoors.

One of the most critical items for outdoor activities is a quality backpack. Depending on the nature of your adventure, you'll want to choose a pack that fits your needs, whether it's a daypack for shorter hikes or a larger backpack for multi-day treks. Look for a pack with adjustable straps and a comfortable fit, as well as features like hydration reservoir sleeves, ample pockets for organization, and rain covers for inclement weather. A good backpack distributes weight evenly, making it easier to carry essential gear without straining your back.

Footwear is another vital consideration when planning outdoor activities. Proper hiking boots or shoes provide the necessary support and traction needed for traversing various terrains. When selecting hiking footwear, consider the type of trails you'll be exploring, as some paths may require more rugged, waterproof boots while others may be more forgiving. It's also important to break in new shoes before hitting the trails to prevent blisters and discomfort.

Layering is key to staying comfortable in Switzerland's variable weather conditions. A well-chosen layering system typically includes a moisture-wicking base layer to keep sweat away from your skin, an insulating mid-layer to retain warmth, and a waterproof or windproof outer layer to protect against rain and wind. Fabrics like merino wool and synthetic materials are excellent choices for base and mid-layers due to their moisture-wicking and insulating properties. Investing in high-quality outdoor clothing will ensure you stay dry and warm while allowing for freedom of movement during your activities.

Accessories such as hats, gloves, and scarves play a significant role in maintaining comfort while engaging in outdoor activities. A wide-brimmed hat can provide sun protection during hikes, while a warm beanie and gloves are essential for winter sports. Buffs or neck gaiters offer versatility, keeping your neck warm while also serving as a face covering against cold winds.

For those planning to engage in water-related activities, such as kayaking or swimming, appropriate gear is necessary. Quick-drying swimwear, water shoes, and rash guards help protect against sunburn and provide comfort in and out of the water. If you plan on kayaking or canoeing, consider bringing a dry bag to keep your belongings safe and dry while you paddle.

When it comes to outdoor equipment, the essentials vary based on your specific activities. Hikers should consider trekking poles, which can help reduce strain on the knees and provide stability on uneven terrain. For climbers, a harness, helmet, and climbing shoes are vital for safety and performance. Skiers and snowboarders require specialized gear, including skis or a snowboard, bindings, and goggles. Renting equipment can be a great option for travelers who may not want to invest in gear for a short visit.

Another important aspect of outdoor gear is navigation tools. While many trails are well-marked, having a reliable map or GPS device can help ensure you stay on course, especially in more remote areas. A portable power bank is also useful for charging devices while out and about, ensuring you have access to navigation apps and emergency communication if needed.

Safety gear should not be overlooked when participating in outdoor activities. A first aid kit, complete with bandages, antiseptics, and other essentials, is crucial for treating minor injuries. If you're venturing into the wilderness or engaging in activities like skiing, consider carrying a whistle, a headlamp or flashlight, and a multi-tool for unexpected situations. In addition, informing someone of your planned route and expected return time is a wise precaution when hiking or exploring remote areas.

Lastly, don't forget to bring a reusable water bottle or hydration system to stay hydrated during your outdoor activities. Maintaining proper hydration is essential, especially during physical exertion at high altitudes. Many areas in Switzerland have clean, drinkable water sources, allowing you to refill your bottle while on the go.

Preparing for outdoor activities in Switzerland requires thoughtful consideration of the right travel gear. Investing in quality equipment tailored to your planned activities can greatly enhance your experience, ensuring you remain comfortable, safe, and able to fully appreciate the stunning natural beauty of the country. With the right gear, you'll be well-equipped to explore the majestic landscapes of Switzerland, whether you are hiking through lush valleys, skiing down snowy slopes, or enjoying the tranquility of a pristine lake.

What to Bring for a Ski Trip

Preparing for a ski trip requires thoughtful consideration of both your gear and personal items to ensure a safe and enjoyable experience on the slopes. Whether you are a beginner or an experienced skier, having the right equipment and essentials can significantly enhance your time on the mountain.

The foundation of your ski attire starts with appropriate clothing. Layering is key for regulating body temperature and staying comfortable throughout the day. Begin with a moisture-wicking base layer that fits snugly against your skin. This layer should draw sweat away from your body, keeping you dry and warm. Look for materials like merino wool or synthetic fabrics designed specifically for cold weather. Your mid-layer should provide insulation, such as a fleece or down jacket, which traps warmth while still allowing breathability.

An outer layer, typically a waterproof and windproof ski jacket and pants, is essential for protection against the elements. These garments should be breathable to allow moisture to escape while keeping you dry from snow and rain. Features like adjustable cuffs, snow skirts, and ventilation zippers can enhance comfort and functionality.

Accessories are crucial for keeping your extremities warm. A good-quality ski helmet is a must for safety, as it protects your head from potential falls and impacts.

Many modern helmets are designed with ventilation systems to prevent overheating. Under the helmet, wear a thin beanie or headband for added warmth.

Ski goggles are another essential piece of gear, providing visibility in various weather conditions and protecting your eyes from harmful UV rays. Choose a pair that fits well and has interchangeable lenses to adapt to changing light conditions. Additionally, a neck gaiter or balaclava is useful for protecting your face from cold winds and snow, while also helping to keep your neck warm.

When it comes to your hands, insulated ski gloves or mittens are necessary to keep your fingers warm and functional. Mittens generally provide more warmth, while gloves offer better dexterity. Look for gloves that are waterproof and breathable, with features like adjustable cuffs and wrist straps to prevent snow from getting inside.

Your feet also need attention, as proper skiing requires good support and warmth. Invest in high-quality ski socks made from merino wool or synthetic materials. These socks should be thick enough to provide cushioning but thin enough to fit comfortably in your ski boots. Avoid cotton socks, as they retain moisture and can lead to cold feet.

If you own your ski equipment, make sure to pack your skis, poles, and boots. Ensure that your boots fit snugly and are comfortable, as proper fitting gear is crucial for performance and safety on the slopes. If you are renting equipment, confirm in advance what will be provided and what you need to bring.

Other important items to consider for your ski trip include sunscreen and lip balm with SPF to protect your skin from the sun's rays, which can be particularly harsh at higher altitudes. Even on cloudy days, UV rays can reflect off the snow, increasing the risk of sunburn. Hydration is also essential, so carry a water bottle or a hydration pack to ensure you stay hydrated throughout the day.

For added convenience, consider bringing a small backpack or ski-specific pack to carry your essentials while on the slopes. This bag can hold snacks, a camera, extra layers, or even your phone for quick access. Make sure it has a secure closure and is designed to be worn comfortably during skiing.

If you're planning to take breaks at mountain lodges or restaurants, packing lightweight clothing like a casual sweater or additional layers can enhance your comfort during downtime. A pair of après-ski shoes, such as warm boots or comfortable sneakers, will make it easier to move around once you're off the slopes.

Additionally, a small first aid kit is always a good idea. Include items such as adhesive bandages, antiseptic wipes, pain relievers, and any personal medications you may need. This preparation can be invaluable in case of minor injuries or ailments that may arise during your trip.

Lastly, don't forget your personal identification, lift tickets, and any necessary travel documents if you are flying to your ski destination. Having everything organized and easily accessible can streamline your arrival and get you on the slopes faster.

In summary, packing for a ski trip involves careful consideration of clothing, accessories, safety gear, and personal items. By being well-prepared, you can focus on enjoying your time on the mountain, making the most of your skiing experience while staying warm, comfortable, and safe.

Made in the USA
Monee, IL
10 January 2025

76519497R00095